The Campus History Series

UNIVERSITY OF
MASSACHUSETTS LOWELL

The Campus History Series

UNIVERSITY OF MASSACHUSETTS LOWELL

MARIE FRANK, PhD

ARCADIA
PUBLISHING

Published by Arcadia Publishing
Charleston, South Carolina

Printed in the United States of America

Library of Congress Catalog Card Number: 2011920357

For all general information, please contact Arcadia Publishing:
Telephone 843-853-2070
Fax 843-853-0044
E-mail sales@arcadiapublishing.com
For customer service and orders:
Toll-Free 1-888-313-2665

Visit us on the Internet at www.arcadiapublishing.com

CONTENTS

ACKNOWLEDGMENTS

This book would not have been possible without the efforts of numerous individuals. First and foremost, I would like to acknowledge the extensive research and scholarship of Prof. Mary Blewett, university historian. Her book, *To Enrich and To Serve: The Centennial History of the University of Massachusetts Lowell* (1995), will remain the authoritative narrative text that draws together the many strands of the university's history. I have relied upon it numerous times. I would also like to thank Martha Mayo at the Center for Lowell History for opening the university archives to me and sharing the results of her own research; Janine Whitcomb scanned all of the historic images with a goodwill for which I will always thank her. Assembling the more recent images proved daunting. Many faculty and university supporters literally took framed photographs off their walls for me. John Ting, Anita Greenwood, Melissa Pennell, Joseph Lipchitz, Aldo Crugnola, John and Catherine Goodwin, Nancy Donohue, Paul Marion, Joe Caulfield, and Dean Bergeron all gave unstintingly of their time. The staff in the Office of Public Affairs provided images of the new buildings; Chris Dunlap wrote the caption for Marty Meehan. Chris O'Donnell and Sean Hladick from the Athletics Department cheerfully guided me through the many student-athlete accomplishments of the last decades. The inimitable Mary Kramer proofed the captions. Finally, I would like to thank Nina Coppens, interim dean of the College of Fine Arts, Humanities and Social Sciences, and Provost Ahmed Abdelal for supporting this project from its beginning. Unless otherwise noted, all images appear courtesy of the University of Massachusetts Lowell Center for Lowell History.

INTRODUCTION

Every place has its own spirit. In the late 18th century, landscape architects used the term *genius loci* (spirit of the place) to describe the special and unique features of a site. Today, Latin phrases are not as common, but historians and planners still seek to identify the "power of place" in their descriptions of communities. This project started out of simple curiosity to understand the "place" that is the University of Massachusetts Lowell (UMass Lowell). For new arrivals—students, faculty, and staff alike—the division between a North Campus and a South Campus (as well as an East and West Campus) presents only the first hurdle. Once on campus, a visitor must distinguish between Olney and Olsen on North; and on South, the even more mystifying confusion of Dugan and Durgin. And if alliteration were not enough, there is the monosyllabic rhyme of Ball Hall and the lilting cadence of O'Leary Library. Who were these people whose names now signify brick and mortar rather than flesh and blood? Other buildings are named for ardent abolitionists (Southwick) or for streets that no longer exist (Falmouth). Floor tiles in Coburn Hall on South depict emblems with torches and musical notes; in Alumni Hall on North, they depict emblems with cotton balls, locks of wool, and shuttles. The buildings themselves hint that the place we call UMass Lowell has a rich and interesting story to tell.

Like Charles Dickens's *A Tale of Two Cities*, the UMass Lowell story is a tale of two schools: the Lowell Normal School on the south side of the Merrimack River and the Lowell Textile School on the north side. Each would follow its own path of expansion into the 20th century. The Normal School, chartered in 1894 and opened in 1897, became Lowell Teachers College in 1932. It opened with 108 students and five faculty members, fought the threat of closure during the Depression, and survived to blossom into Lowell State College in 1960 with a curriculum expanded beyond education courses to include baccalaureate degrees in the liberal arts. Lowell Textile School, approved in 1895, opened in 1897 in rented rooms in downtown Lowell, but soon amassed the resources for an impressive complex of three buildings (Southwick, Kitson, and Falmouth) on an open site next to the Merrimack River. The "school" became Lowell Textile Institute in 1928, but also suffered during the Depression and World War II (enrollment dipped to a senior class of 12 in 1945). In the postwar years, passage of the GI Bill filled the classrooms, and a curriculum that expanded beyond textiles into other industries necessitated the new name of Lowell Technological Institute (LTI) in 1953. In 1975, the two institutions finally merged to become the University of Lowell, and then merged again with the University of Massachusetts system in 1991. Today, the university offers its 15,000 students more than 120 different degrees, along with internships, co-ops, five-year combined bachelor's to master's programs, and doctoral studies in the colleges of Fine Arts, Humanities and Social Sciences, Sciences, Engineering, and Management, the School of Health and Environment, and the Graduate School of Education.

The extensive collection of historic photographs as well as the amply illustrated yearbooks testified to a spirit, strong and identifiable, that remained steadfast through all of the school's various incarnations. The journey through these resources at the UMass Lowell Center for Lowell History has been uplifting and humbling at the same time. The yearbooks—the *Knoll* for the Teachers College and the *Pickout* for Lowell Textile—convey a palpable enthusiasm for new endeavors. Many of the current student activities are rooted in long traditions. The student newspaper, the *Connector*, had its precursor in the *Campus Star*; production of Shakespeare's plays began as early as 1905; Chinese students started a club in the late 1920s; and women played field hockey behind Coburn Hall in the 1930s. The two signature buildings of each campus, Coburn Hall on South and Southwick on North, reveal the confidence and pride that surrounded these new endeavors. Both employ a quality of design, materials, and construction that went beyond the mere utilitarian. Coburn had New Hampshire granite steps, custom-fitted golden oak paneling, brass light fixtures, copper gutters with carved lion's-head fixtures, and large spacious rooms that freed the thoughts and ideas of students. Upon completion of each building, administrators hired professional photographers to document the structures using large format negatives.

And then there are the people—the faculty, staff, and administrators who worked at either one or both institutions for decades. Charles Eames led the Textile Institute for almost four decades; Herbert Ball, a mechanical engineer, taught for 48 years; Ruth Foote served as registrar at LTI from 1913 until the 1940s; Dean Bergeron started teaching in 1968 and still teaches one class a year; Waldo "Rusty" Yarnall coached and directed the Athletics Department for over 40 years; Joseph Collins ran the boiler house on North for 40 years; DeMerritte Hiscoe taught art for over 30 years; Robert "Bobby" Desruisseaux shoveled and salted the steps of Coburn through endless winters; and Alice Conlon had a ready smile for all in Dining Services. The memories of many of these people may only remain in photographs, but their energy and expertise shaped the physical and educational character of the place called UMass Lowell.

For all the diverse accomplishments of the people and programs represented in the photographs here, there are undoubtedly an equal number that are not. This volume in no way attempts to present a complete and thorough account of the university's history. By its very nature, a project like this relies on a visual record of photographs and digital images; an absence of publication-quality images has left many noteworthy events unrepresented. The presence of the past is fragile—it can depend upon a dusty framed photograph propped against a wall in an obscure closet or stashed in a darkened basement. A number of the images in this book were rescued by Tony Sampas and other observant individuals. We must also continue to take good, high-quality images of the present. One of the ironies of the digital age is that taking a photograph has become so easy that we pay less attention to the quality of the shot—the framing, lighting, composition, or level of detail. If this book can encourage readers to preserve the photographs they have and take better ones in the future, the effort of assembling it will be well rewarded.

One

TEACHING TEACHERS

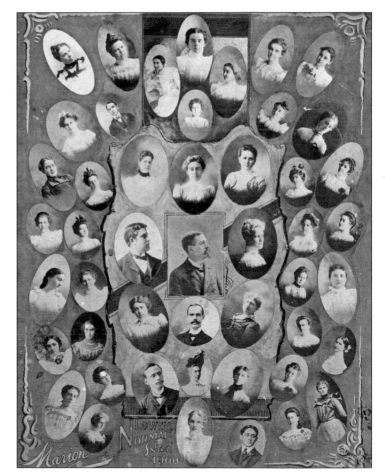

In 1894, the Lowell School Committee and city council convinced the State Board of Education and legislature to locate a normal school in the city. The term "normal" had its antecedents in France's École Normale Superiore; these schools prepared students for teaching careers through a two-year curriculum based upon current standards, or "norms." The school opened in the fall of 1897; this image depicts the faculty and class of 1900.

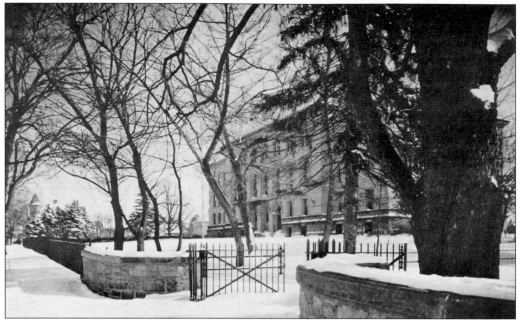

The city provided $25,000 for the new building and, in consultation with prominent Lowellian Charles Allen, selected a site at the corner of Broadway and Wilder Streets in Allen's own neighborhood near the Merrimack River. The school soon became a landmark in the city. Designed by the local firm of Stickney and Austin, it reflects the fashion of the times—high-style Beaux Arts design with classical symmetry, arches, cast-iron lampposts, lion's-head-adorned gutters, and a dignified bearing. Frederick Stickney, a native of Lowell who attended MIT, also designed Lowell High School. Many students arrived at school via the trolley that ran along Broadway (the tracks are just visible in the cover photograph). The lampposts, along with the cast-iron railing added later, were unfortunately removed after the mid-1970s.

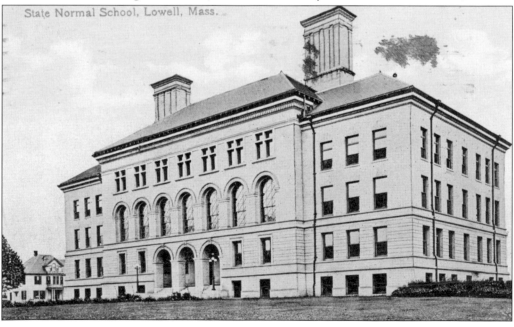

Frank Coburn served as the first principal of the Lowell Normal School, from 1897 to 1907. He was a specialist in physics and geology and had extensive experience in the Lowell public school system, having served as head of Lowell High School. In 1898, a back injury paralyzed his legs but did not deter him from efficiently overseeing the curriculum. Coburn Hall was named in his honor in 1975.

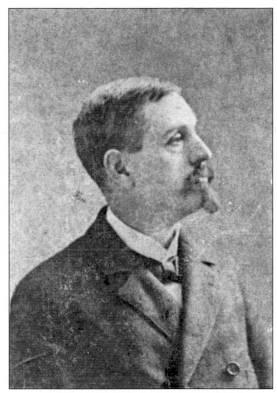

The 1897 academic year opened with an enrollment of 108 students—105 women and 3 men. The students took courses in educational methods (initially taught by Frank Coburn) as well as English, mathematics, science, and drawing. By 1898, Coburn had five faculty members, a secretary who also served as librarian, a physical education instructor, and two maintenance men.

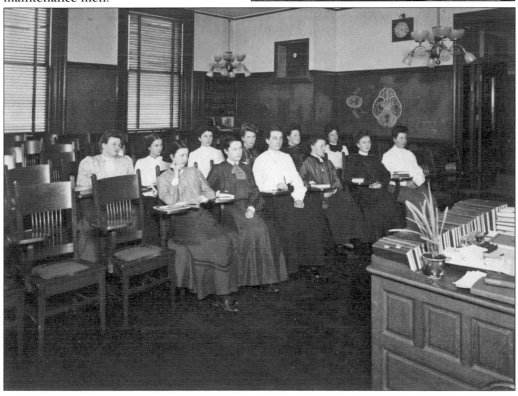

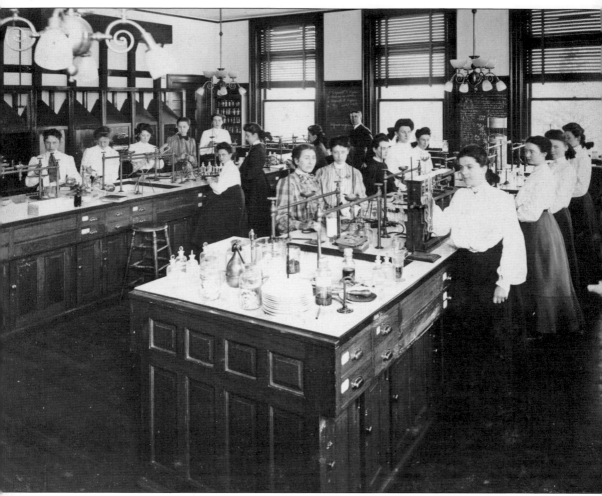

The classrooms were fitted with the latest equipment. By 1905, students studied chemistry and conducted experiments in an impressive laboratory in one of the third-floor classrooms. Standing at the back of the room is the chemistry professor, Dr. Lyman C. Newell. Although Newell left Lowell after a few years for Boston University, his courses set the sciences on firm footing.

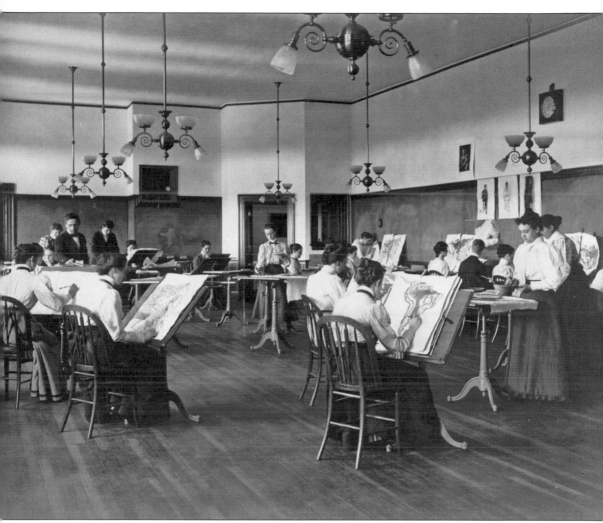

Additional courses in the sciences included classes in geography, mineralogy, and botany. Geography was taught by Walter J. Kenyon, who also taught drawing. Here, students use the north light of the large drawing room on the third floor as they sketch and map the geography of South America. The adjustable desktops could also serve as easels for art classes.

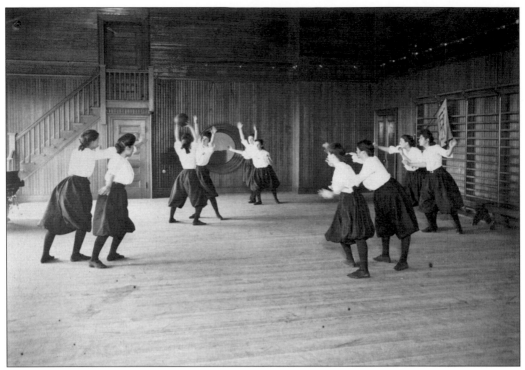

Today, students are often surprised to hear that the third floor of Coburn Hall once held a gymnasium. It occupied space over the large assembly room on the second floor. Gym class offered women a short respite from the hours spent in corsets and high collars; classes typically began with deep-breathing exercises. Basketball, invented in 1891, immediately became popular. No one was allowed to hold the ball longer than three seconds; this picture shows the women, sporting the full bloomers deemed proper, working the ball toward the basket over the circular window. The stairs at each end of the gym led to attic space that contained marble showers.

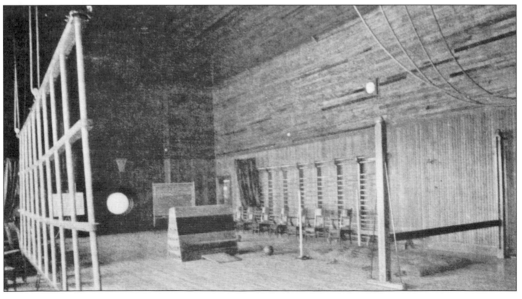

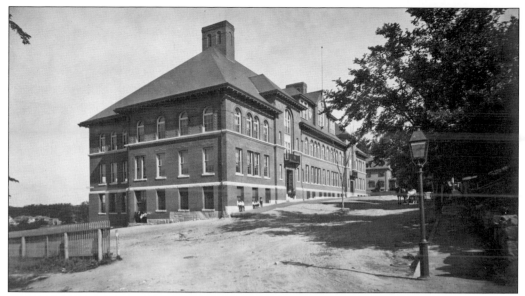

Perhaps the most critical part of the curriculum centered on student teaching. The Bartlett Training School, located a few blocks away from Coburn Hall on Wannalancit Street, served as the training and practice facility for Normal School students. Beginning in their second term, each student spent a week at the Bartlett; in their third terms, they spent the entire semester there. The principal of the school, Cyrus A. Durgin, not only oversaw a large elementary school, he also had to accommodate the student-trainees. Trainees began by simply observing classes but eventually had the opportunity to conduct classes on their own, such as this outdoor sketching class taking place near "Francis' Folly," the lock on the Pawtucket Canal. When Frank Coburn died in early 1908, Durgin became the second principal of the Normal School.

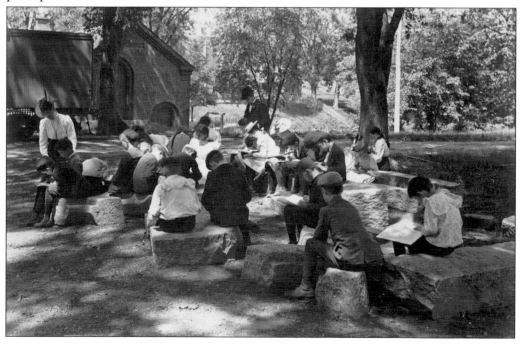

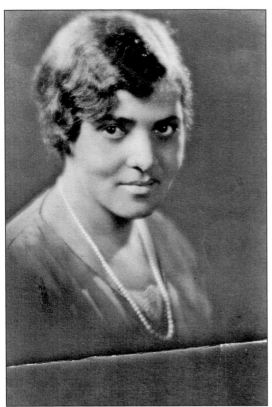

Teresa Garland Lew stands out as one of the school's most remarkable early students. After becoming the first African American graduate of the school in 1914, she went on to earn a law degree from Portia Law School in Boston while simultaneously working at the Bartlett Training School. Teresa's sister Marion completed the new music program instituted by Durgin, and their niece enrolled at Lowell Technological Institute. (Courtesy of Gerard Ashe.)

Wearing the white dresses traditional for graduation, a group of students gathered behind Coburn Hall for a photograph in 1916. From left to right are (first row) Ruth Tingley, Nelle Horner, and Lotta Warley; (second row) Zilpha Wallace, Blanche Spalding, Freda White, Bessie Browne, and Hazel Stevens. Clarence Weed had landscaped the area with shrubs and roses; the house visible in the distance is now owned by UMass Lowell.

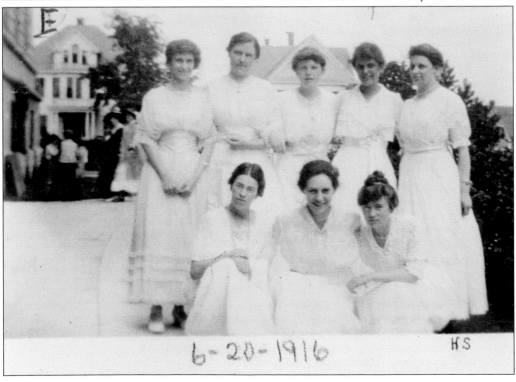

6-20-1916   HS

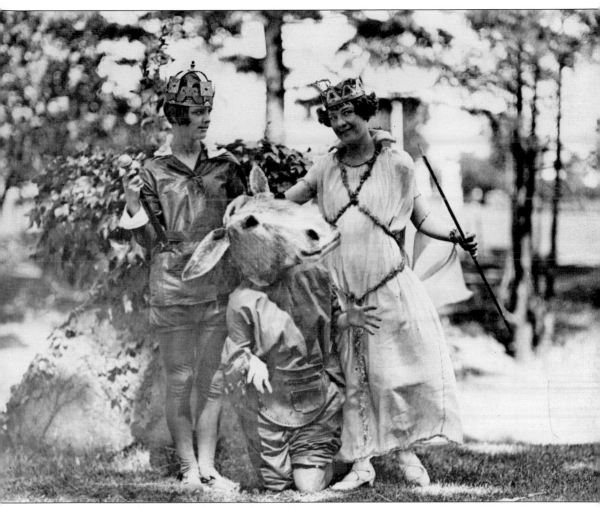

The theater arts have had a long and active history on campus. As early as 1905, students performed both for classmates and for the children at the Bartlett, designing elaborate costumes and props for plays such as Shakespeare's *A Midsummer Night's Dream*. Here, Titania and Oberon flank a very convincing Bottom c. 1905.

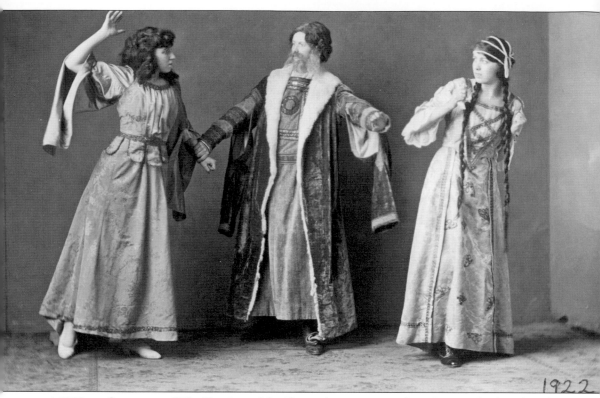

1922

A 1922 performance of *The Taming of the Shrew* demonstrates that, despite the fact that the school had a few male students, productions often ran with all-female casts—the dark hair of the tall actress at center contradicts her gray, grizzled fake beard.

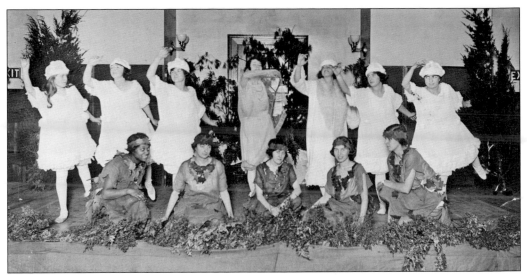

Not all performances centered on established playwrights. Each year, the juniors and seniors put on a reception that involved short sketches, dances, and musical performances. Faculty sometimes participated as well. A scene from the reception of 1919 is pictured above. In the 1925 academic year, however, students returned to Shakespeare with a vengeance, pouring their efforts into "Merry Masque of Shakespeare," an event that featured a compilation of scenes from over eight of his plays. Pictured below are members of the cast of *The Merry Wives of Windsor*. Florence Kirby, hired under Weed in the 1920s to teach storytelling techniques, was the long-serving faculty advisor to the drama club until her retirement in 1948.

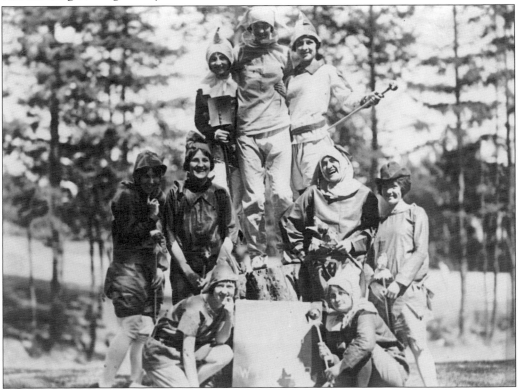

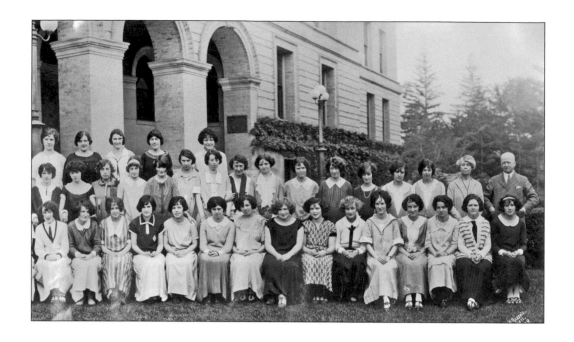

The above image—half of a panorama of the class of 1924—includes Blanche Cheney and Clarence Weed at far right, second row. Cheney, hired in 1909, taught history and served as dean until 1944. Weed, a scientist, succeeded John J. Mahoney as fourth principal of the school in 1922. Unlike Mahoney, whose tenure from 1916 to 1922 was marked by long absences, Weed had a major impact on the curriculum. He avidly searched for and embraced new pedagogical methods and in 1932 managed the transition of the Normal School into the four-year Lowell Teachers College. A large stained-glass window with the letters "LTC," installed at the main entrance to Coburn Hall, remains in place today. Weed retired in 1935. In the 1946 image below, students gather around the sign that denoted the status of the college.

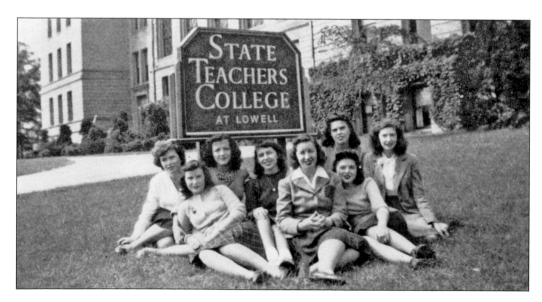

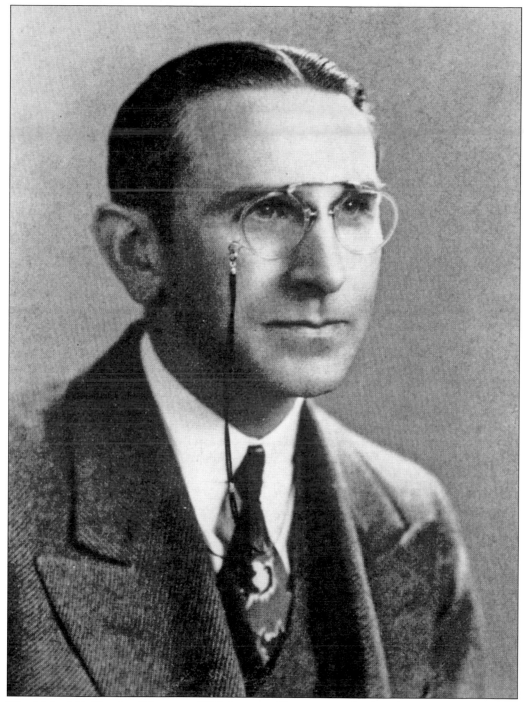

Weed hired DeMerritte Hiscoe in 1925 for one of his more radical pedagogical innovations: he wanted Hiscoe, a trained artist, to teach students how to sketch images of any subject quickly on the blackboard as an aid in teaching. The students dedicated the first yearbook, *The 'Marm* of 1934, to Hiscoe, and he remained a popular teacher into the 1960s.

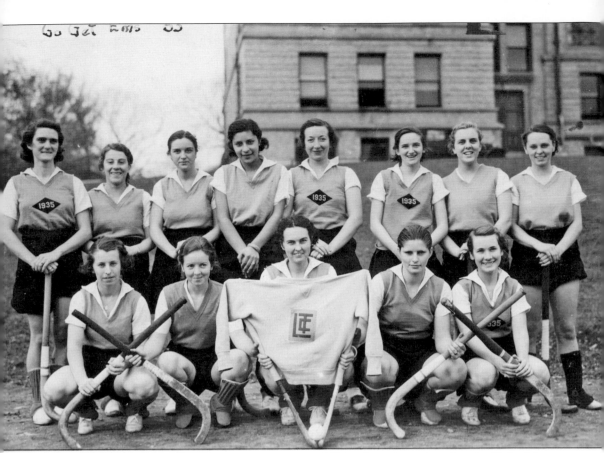

Women's field hockey started in Great Britain in 1887 and was introduced to the United States in 1901, where it flourished. The physical demands of speed and endurance required in the game suggest that this 1933 team (displaying the new LTC logo) included some of the best athletes in the college. The team played against other schools in the area, and its members also participated in a popular intramural competition that pitted class against class.

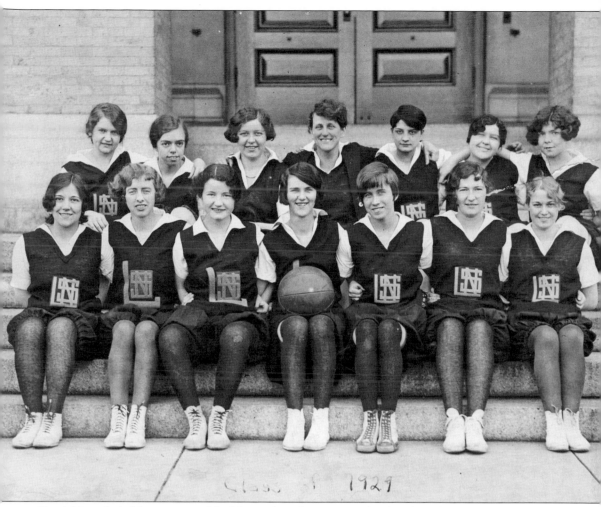

Class of 1929

Banishing their bloomers and bobbing their hair, Normal School students retained their passion for basketball. The 1929 team depicted here benefited from the effort, in 1928, to establish a national standard of official rules for women's basketball. Ruth Bailey, the long-serving physical education instructor and an outstanding basketball player in her own right, may be at the center of the second row. She retired in 1935.

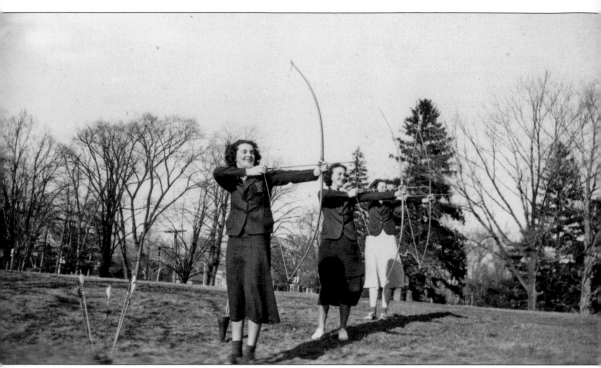

Archery, long accepted as a suitable outdoor activity for women, gained prestige when women were allowed to compete in the 1904 Olympics. Into the 1940s, archery offered LTC students an alternative to the more physical sports of basketball and field hockey. As the authors of the 1935 *Knoll* claimed: "The Athletic Association is one of the most important organizations in the college. Its membership includes practically the entire student body."

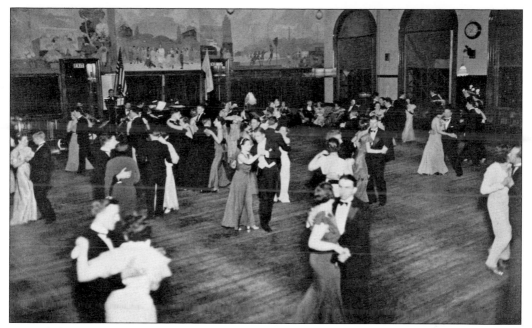

Formal dances punctuated the academic calendar. For the 1934 junior prom, students transformed the assembly room of Coburn Hall, decorating the space with ivy-strewn pillars and Japanese lanterns for "four of the happiest hours of our college life." Each spring, student government organized a college-wide formal; at the 1936 event, couples dance below newly painted Works Progress Administration (WPA) murals that ring the room.

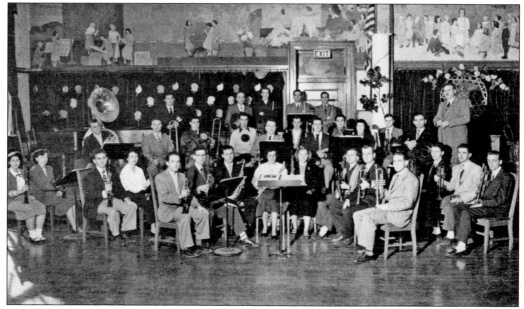

This group photograph of the orchestra from the 1952 *Knoll* inadvertently gives a good sense of what the murals in Coburn looked like. Depression-era artists, working under the New Deal's WPA program, were frequently hired to paint murals in public institutional buildings. The artist is not known, but the style and subject matter are typical for the period. All of the murals were painted over by the early 1970s.

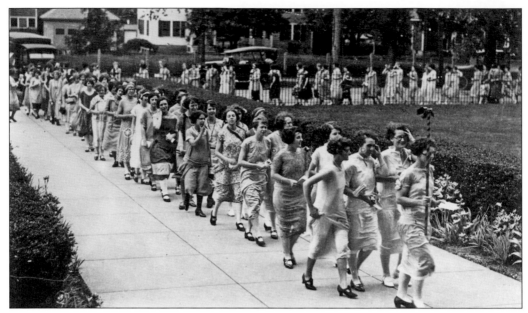

By the 1930s, Coburn Hall (shown below) had aged with grace; ivy adorned its foundation and the trees had grown in. As the only school building, it was used for everything. The above image depicts Normal School commencement exercises in 1931, the last year before its change in status to a college. These students, processing into Coburn Hall on a windy day, represent one of the last groups to receive two-year degrees; they were also the last group of students to arrive at school by trolley. Following the national pattern, Lowell cut back on public transportation—the trolley made its last run up Broadway Street on September 26, 1930. The resulting dependence on automobile transportation increased parking demands that have not ceased to this day.

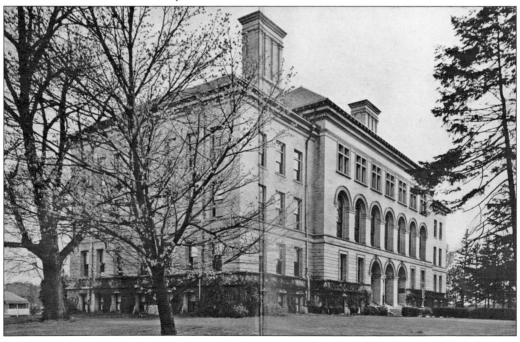

Two

AN EDUCATION
FOR INDUSTRY

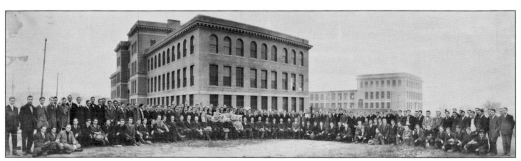

This c. 1903 panorama depicts the trustees, faculty, and students of Lowell Textile School in front of the newly completed buildings along the Merrimack River—Southwick (behind the group), Falmouth (parallel to Southwick), and Kitson (not visible; perpendicular to both). The road now known as Veterans' Foreign Wars Highway (VFW) is literally a dirt road and the building, now known as Pasteur, that closed the quad was not dedicated until 1938.

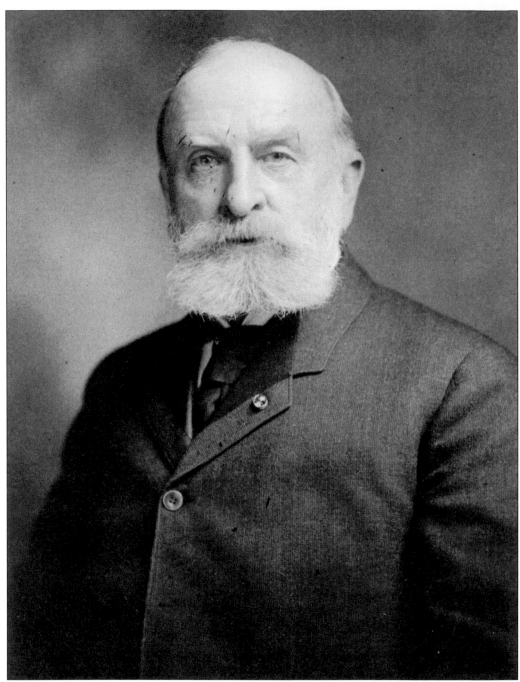

In the wake of the early 1890s depression, James T. Smith, secretary to the Lowell Board of Trade, unremittingly lobbied the state legislature to locate a semiprivate textile school in Lowell. As part of a larger effort to make the United States competitive in the European textile market, schools like the one in Lowell focused on increasing the skills of textile employees while also exploring new technologies. The school, approved in 1895, had close ties with the mill men who were expected to provide financial support and serve on the governing board. Smith, acknowledged as the school's founder, remained its guiding force.

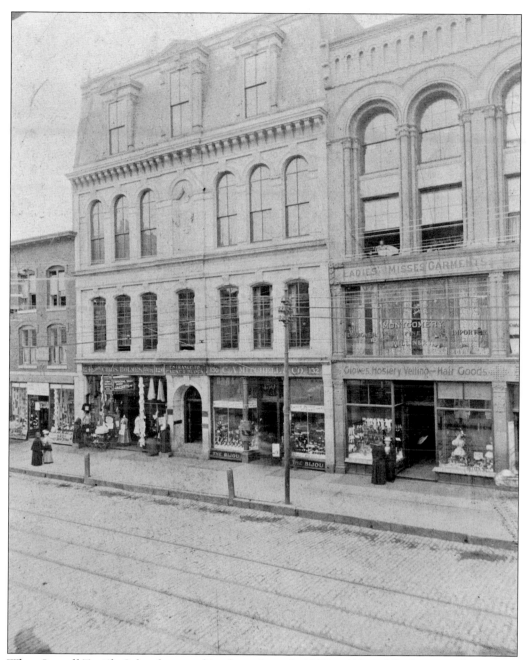

When Lowell Textile School opened its doors in early 1897 at 128 Middle Street in downtown Lowell, it offered a three-year diploma to day students and free night classes for textile workers. Four areas of study were available: cotton manufacturing, wool manufacturing, textile design, and textile chemistry.

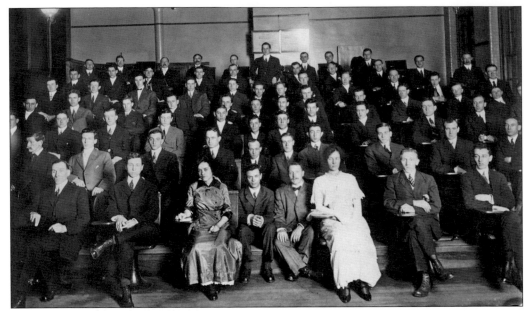

This image may depict the first class of students in 1897. Two Victorian-garbed women sit amongst a sea of over 40 male students—the complete inverse of the gender ratio across the river at the Normal School. By 1901–1902, the school listed a "Women's Department" that combined decorative art and textile design. Through the 1960s, women remained a minority within the student body at Lowell Textile.

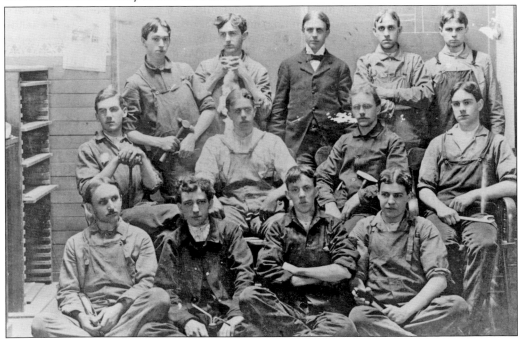

Members of the class of 1900 pictured here underscore the practical aims of the curriculum. As noted in the school's bulletin, the course of studies was taught "not with the object of educating professional scientific men, but with a view to industrial and commercial applications." The students wear overalls and hold hammers, wrenches, and bobbins.

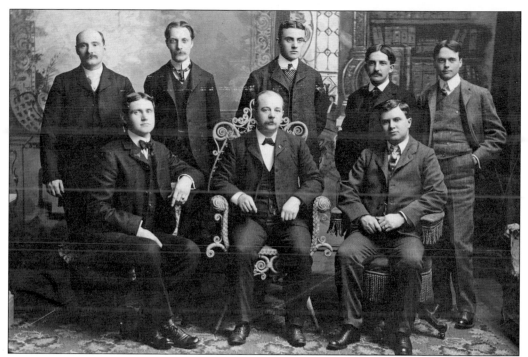

Prof. Fenwick Umpleby, seated at the center and surrounded by students in 1901, was typical of the highly trained faculty that Smith brought to Lowell. Umpleby headed the textile design department and soon wrote a number of books, including *Textile Design and Cloth Analysis*. In 1910, he described himself as the "Chief of the Departments of Cloth Construction, Design, Analysis and Weaving." His success gained him attention outside of Lowell, and by 1912, he left to become principal at the competing Bradford Durfee Textile School in Fall River (which, in an interesting twist of history, later became part of UMass Dartmouth). The design department classroom he most likely used at the Middle Street location is pictured below.

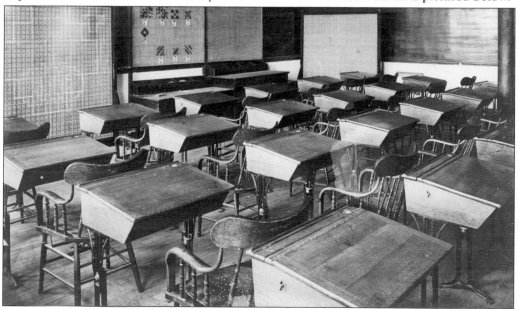

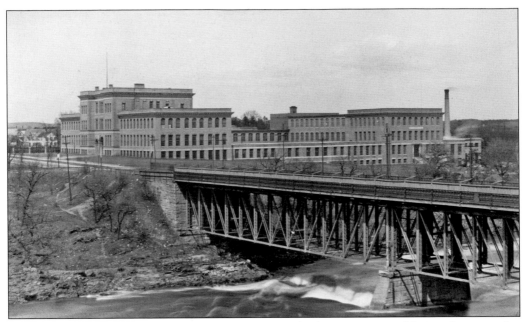

Smith's ambitions for the school included a purpose-built institution. Lobbying the state, city, and citizens, he secured funding for three buildings on a plot of land next to the Merrimack River and a bridge that maintained the school's connection with the mills. Frederick Fanning Ayer gave $100,000 for the main building, stipulating it be named for his maternal grandfather, Royal Southwick. Falmouth, positioned parallel to Southwick, took its name from an existing street that ran behind it (and which no longer exists). The third building, Kitson (visible in the below image at far left, two stories), was a gift from the daughters of Richard Kitson, founder of the Kitson Machine Company in Lowell. The plot also included five acres of playing fields adjacent to Kitson. All three buildings were in use by 1903.

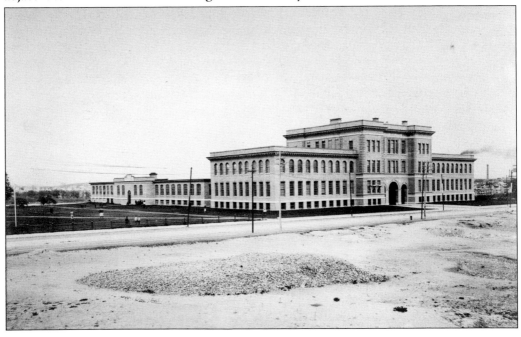

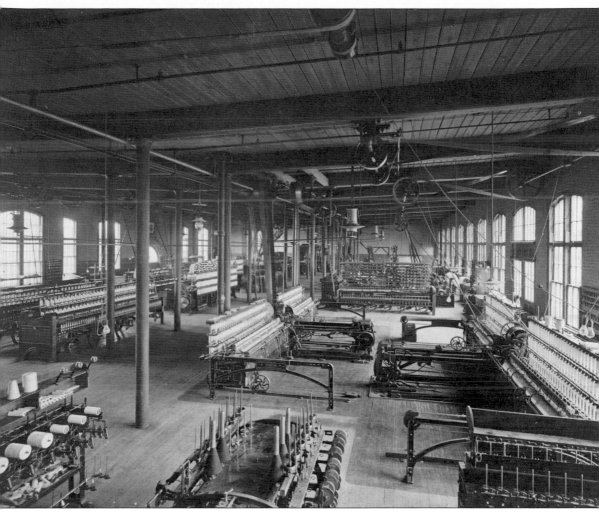

Kitson contained the cotton yarn department. As this image suggests, many of the classrooms were indistinguishable from working mills. Students learned by working directly with the machinery. The buildings themselves also mirrored the mills—the school bulletin proudly proclaimed that "the basis of all the buildings is mill construction." Kitson was designed by Boston architects and engineers Lockwood Greene & Company.

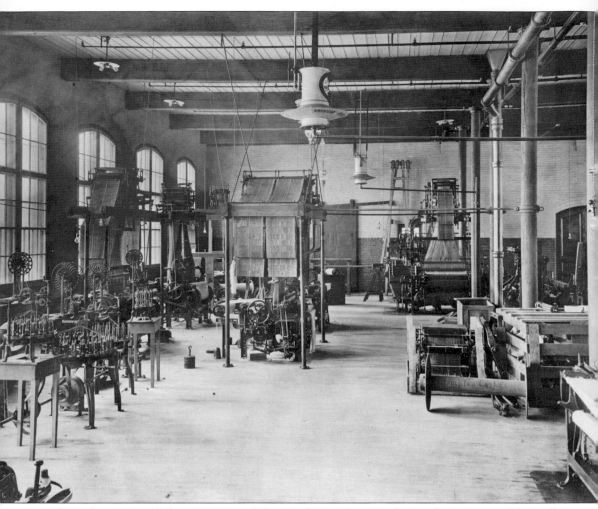

Falmouth contained the weaving and the woolen and worsted yarn departments. The mill construction praised in the school bulletin is clearly visible in this picture, with bobbin winders at right and a power loom in the back. By 1911, hand looms occupied the top floor, a space shared with the design department offices and a large classroom.

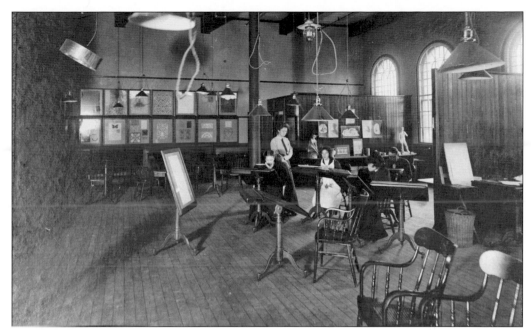

The decorative art department, pictured below around 1903, differed slightly from the other departments because it attracted a wider range of students. Run by Vesper George, a trained artist, it prepared students for design work in any branch of the decorative arts—not just textile design. This openness found a ready market as the Arts and Crafts movement gained momentum nationally; many design students went on to apply these skills to ceramics, metalwork, or stained glass. Women in particular, like those in the classroom above, pursued artisanal careers. George eventually left Lowell to found the Vesper George School of Art in Boston.

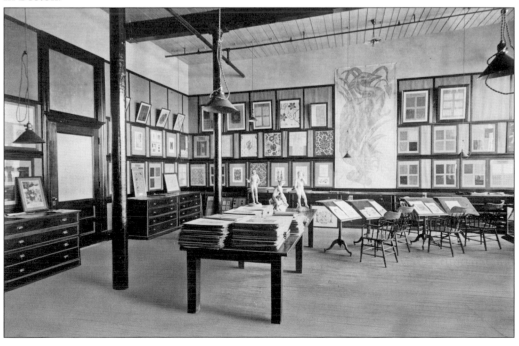

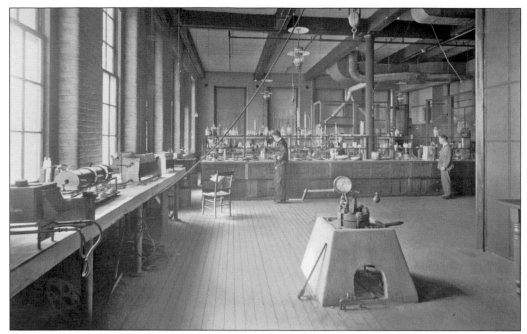

Louis Atwell Olney ran the chemistry and dyeing department and had no hesitation in proclaiming its (and his) importance. The ability to consistently dye fibers was essential to the success of the textile market. The famous French tapestry firm of Gobelins had hired the notable chemist M.E. Chevreul earlier in the century, and Olney saw himself in the same light. He demanded the best equipment, the best space, and special woodwork in his private laboratory. He was later joined in the department by Elmer Fickett, in 1917, and Frederick Beattie by the mid-1920s (Beattie taught organic chemistry; his lab is pictured below). Olney vied to become principal of the school but lost to Charles Eames.

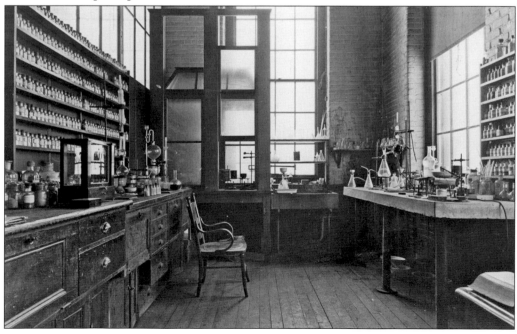

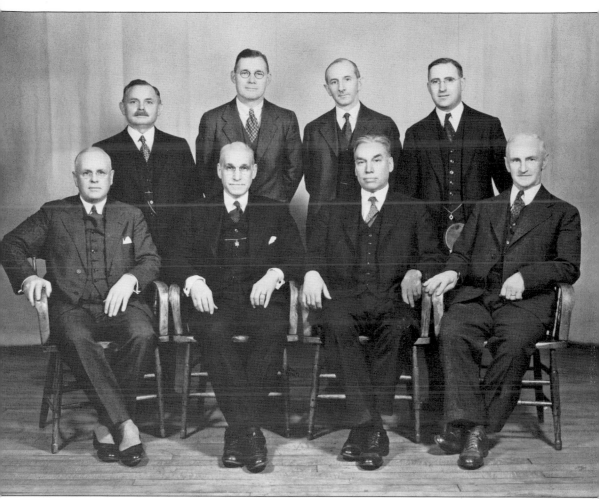

In 1906, Charles H. Eames became the second principal of the Lowell Textile School, a position he held for the next 39 years. Eames was photographed in February 1934 with other long-standing faculty who shaped the school. From left to right are (first row) Arthur A. Stewart, Louis A. Olney, Eames, and Edgar H. Barker; (second row) Hermann H. Bachmann, Lester H. Cushing, Herbert J. Ball, and Gilbert R. Merrill.

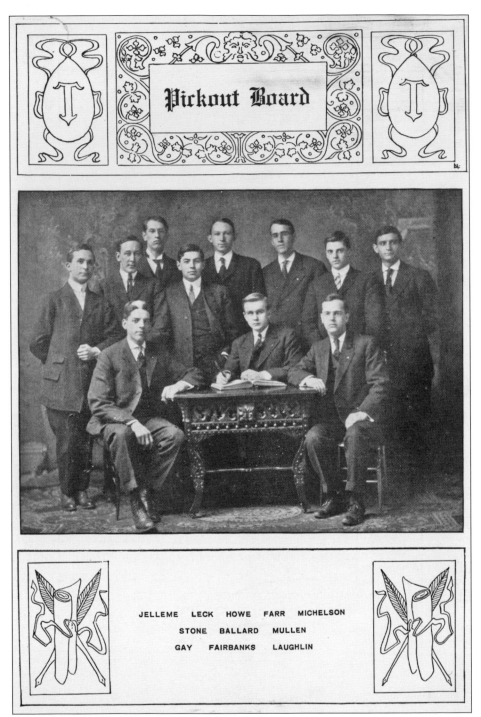

Pickout Board

JELLEME LECK HOWE FARR MICHELSON

STONE BALLARD MULLEN

GAY FAIRBANKS LAUGHLIN

With the enthusiasm that marks many new ventures, students quickly began a yearbook to highlight their years at Textile. The first issue appeared in 1906; they titled it the *Pickout*, a term used in the textile industry to describe individual weft threads drawn forward or "picked-out" from an overall pattern. The yearbook continued under that name until the 1975 merger, when the name was changed to *Sojourn*.

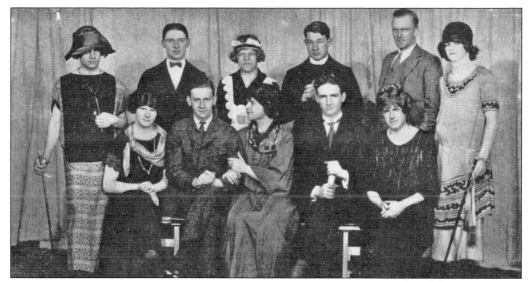

Also in 1906, students started production of an annual Textile Show to raise money for the athletic association. The show consisted of songs, monologues, and sketches that brought out the creativity of the otherwise practical-minded students. In 1907, two students wrote and performed a humorous sketch about a newly married couple. As this image suggests, even though the student body included women, the female roles were played by men.

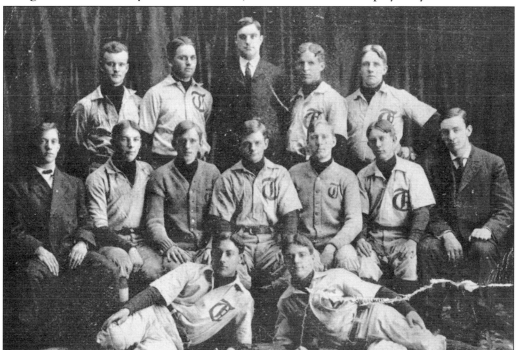

From the school's opening in 1897, students played a variety of sports, including baseball, basketball, and football. Baseball claimed to be the oldest of the school's sports although it was admittedly not initially a "howling success," according to *Pickout* editors. The 1905 team pictured here was the first to gain renown. They played nine games and had three losses; the team's biggest rival at the time was Lowell High School.

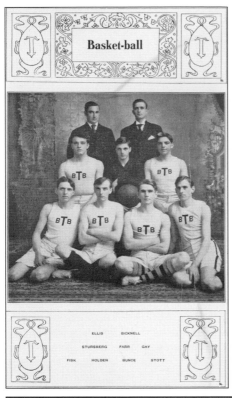

Basket-ball

ELLIS BICKNELL

STURSBERG FARR GAY

FISK HOLDEN BUNCE STOTT

Students tried to form a basketball team in 1901 but had no place to practice until Southwick opened in 1903. A gymnasium was located on the fourth floor, and despite the awkward low ceilings and cast-iron columns, the team surged forward. In the 1905–1906 season, the team pictured here played 17 games, only losing to Andover Academy and defeating Boston College, Brown, Dartmouth, and Boston University, among others. The national passion for collegiate football prompted students to field a team as early as 1902. The 1908 team pictured below displays the determination necessary for survival. Without the forward pass, games in this period were low-scoring and much more violent—formations such as the famed "Flying Wedge," although officially banned, were still used and frequently resulted in broken bones and concussions. The team's schedule in 1908 included games against Tufts, Worcester Polytech, and MIT.

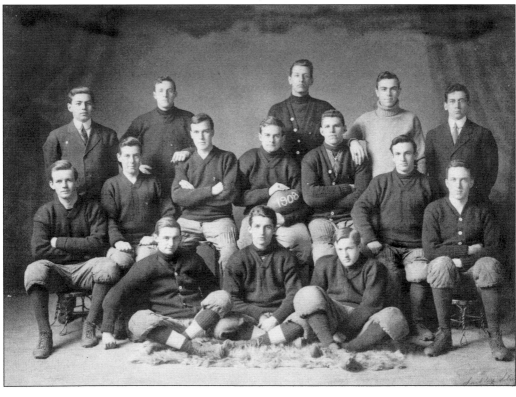

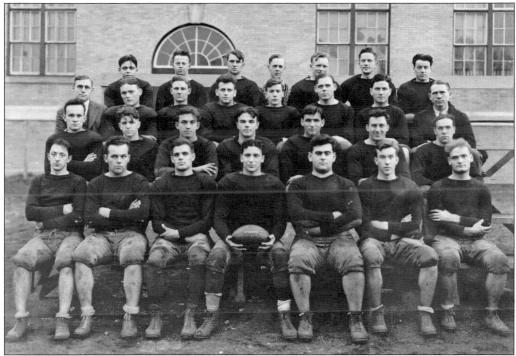

The 1928 football team had a perfect season and became the first unbeaten team in Lowell Textile School's collegiate varsity history. The captain of the team, Herman Gross, is holding the ball in the first row. At each end of the third row are two of the most important figures in the school's athletic history: the famed coach Waldo "Rusty" Yarnall (right) and Lester Cushing. Yarnall coached baseball, basketball, and football. Cushing, hired in 1911 to teach languages and history, quickly migrated into the position of athletics director and remained there until 1960; Yarnall succeeded him until his retirement in 1973. The fields outside of Kitson were multipurpose; in the below image, the baseball team plays with the football goal posts (visible at left) still on the field.

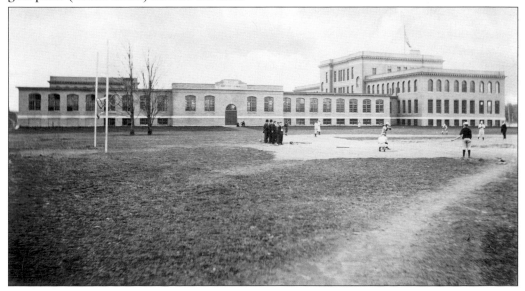

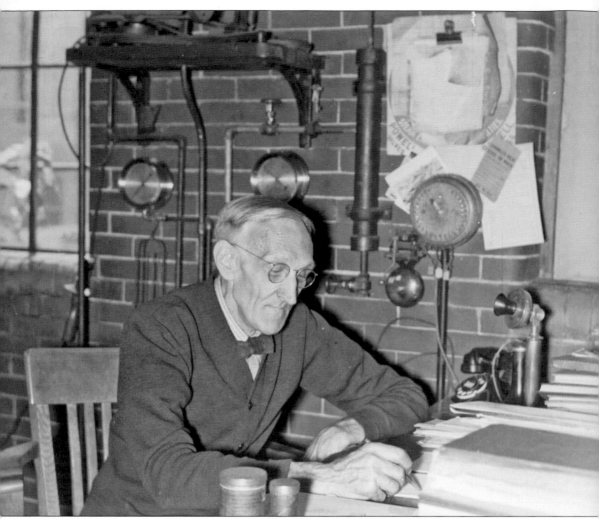

Joseph Collins served as the chief engineer of the boiler plant on campus for an impressive four decades—from the opening of Southwick in 1902 until his retirement in 1942. Collins lived on Varney Street in the Acre neighborhood of Lowell and walked to work each day. The boiler building served as the unofficial entry to campus after hours, when the gate in Southwick was locked up.

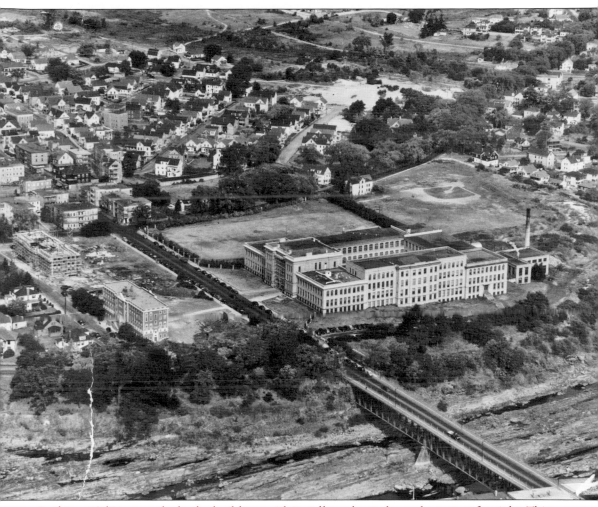

In this c. 1947 image, the boiler building, with its tall smokestack, can be seen at far right. This aerial photograph was taken shortly after the completion of Smith and Eames dormitories and before the construction of the Alumni Memorial Library and Cumnock Hall.

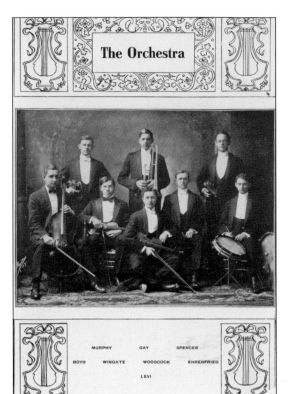

The Orchestra

MURPHY   GAY   SPENCER

BOYD   WINGATE   WOODCOCK   EHRENFRIED

LEVI

Students with musical skills formed an orchestra and a mandolin and guitar club that performed throughout the year. In addition, a number of members also accompanied the Textile Show skits. Under the management of chemistry professor Elmer Fickett, the annual Textile Show grew into a bigger and more elaborate undertaking in the 1920s. As enthusiasm for acting increased, students formed the Textile Players and added the performance of full-length plays to the show's offerings. The graphic below announces the production of *The Philadelphia Story*, a popular Broadway hit that was later turned into a movie starring Katharine Hepburn and Cary Grant. Only after World War II did the Players' productions include females.

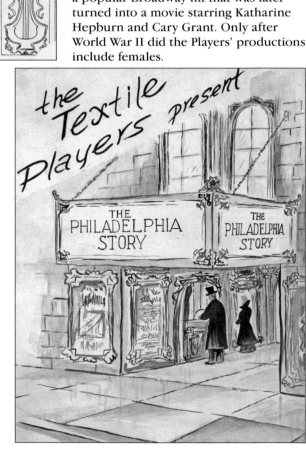

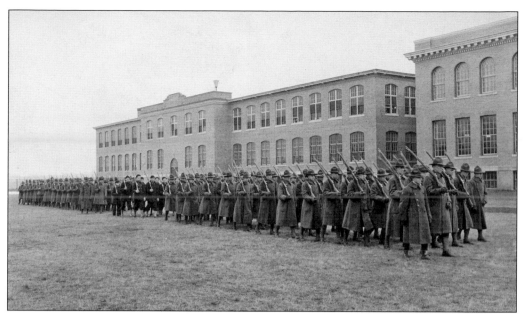

Both world wars had a direct impact on the institution. In World War I, the playing fields outside of Kitson were frequently used as part of a training camp for Army recruits. In 1947, after World War II, the bridge over the Merrimack, which had gone through a number of names, was designated as "Textile Memorial Bridge" in honor of classmates killed in the war, including Donald M. Adie, Joseph H. Berkowitz, Thomas W. Broderick, Thomas F. Cryan, H. Russell Cunningham, Philip C. Evans, Burgess C. Harpoot, Roger H. Kane, Edwin J. Kozera, Martin P. Murray, Walter H. Paige Jr., Richard I. Parthum, Samuel Pearsall, Kilburn G. Pease, Ernest M. Stromvall, and Frederick L. Webster.

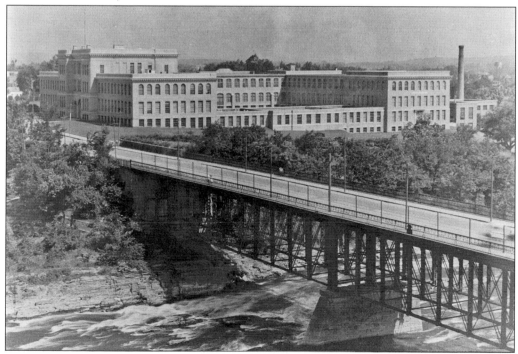

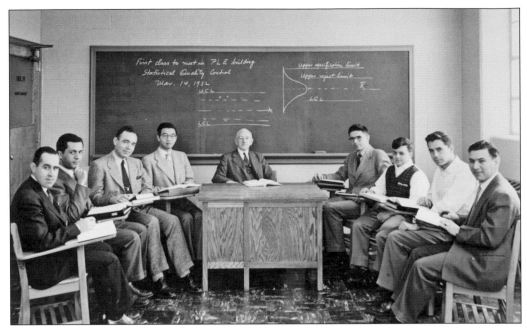

The hiring of faculty like mechanical engineer Herbert Ball in 1907 signaled a transition in the curriculum from training operatives to production engineering—that is, greater attention to studies that increased production efficiency. Ball, who taught at the school into the 1950s, is shown above on March 14, 1952, in the center of the first class taught in the new Paper and Leather Engineering Building (now known as the Engineering Building). In 1928, Lowell Textile School was officially renamed Lowell Textile Institute. Textiles remained the emphasis, however, as shown by the 1930s exhibit of Woolen and Worsted Manufacturing pictured below. It featured different types of wool (such as cashmere) but also blends (worsted and rayon nub, rabbit, and silk), and types of yarn (French spun and Jasper yarn). Only after World War II did the curriculum begin to embrace other industries.

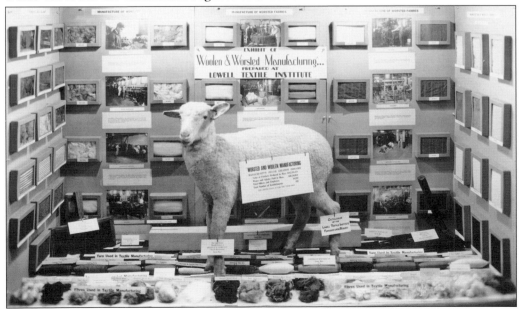

Three

EXPANSION ALONG THE MERRIMACK

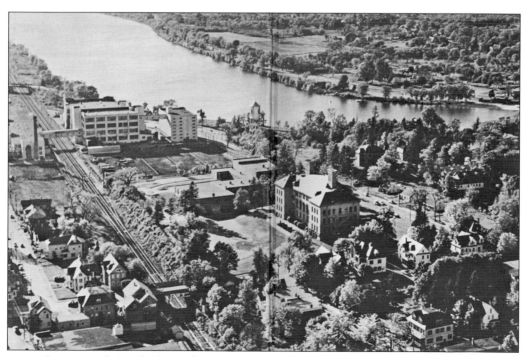

From the 1930s through the 1960s, Teachers College continued to expand. In this aerial image from the 1957 *Knoll*, Coburn Hall is still situated within the residential neighborhood of Wilder and Broadway Streets but is now flanked by Mahoney Hall. A mill, operated by the Bay State Cotton Corporation, occupied what is now the student parking lot. The area on the opposite side of the river was open farmland.

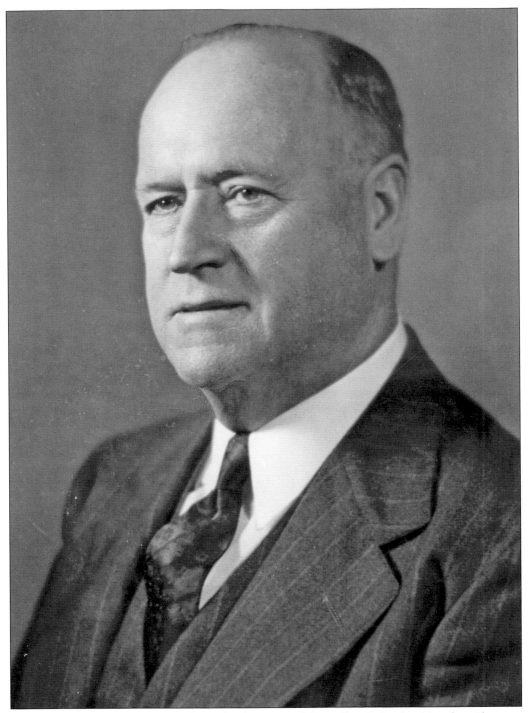

James M. Dugan arrived in 1936 to take the reins of the college's leadership after Clarence Weed's retirement. Dugan served as president of Lowell State Teachers College until 1950 and worked diligently to expand the student body, faculty, and programs; he also banished some of the more rigid rules. His decisions undoubtedly helped transform the institution at a pivotal period and ultimately increased its collegiate atmosphere.

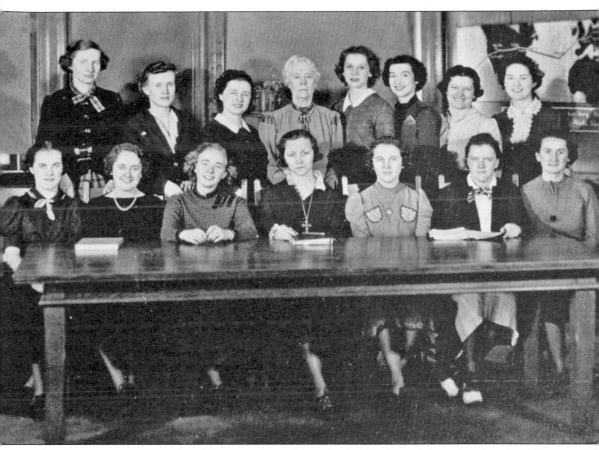

Student government existed in some form from the beginning of the school and took a more definite shapc by the 1930s (the 1937 officers are pictured). Initially called the School and Society League, the group met once a week to "try to solve" students' problems. Dean Blanche Cheney served as the faculty advisor. By the 1950s, the group's name was changed to the Student Government Association.

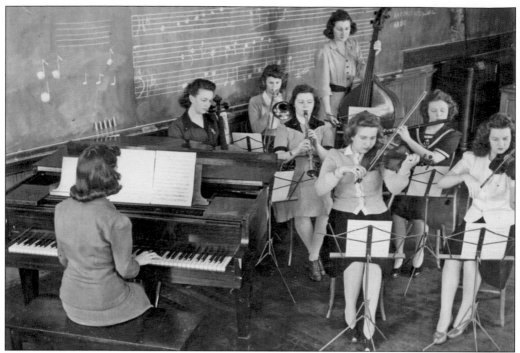

From the start, music had a seminal place in the curriculum. In 1912, the school offered a one-year program to train music supervisors, and following the transformation into a four-year college in 1932, students had the option to major in music education. The students also performed regularly in choirs, orchestras, and bands. Indeed, in the 1940s, the same students often participated in all three—members of the swing band called it the "most flexible band in the land." Classical music served as an anchor within the curriculum, but the swing band, pictured below around 1944, allowed students to indulge their love of Gershwin and other contemporary composers. In the 1950s, the music program grew under the direction of Edward F. Gilday and popular faculty members such as Domenic Procopio. A performance major was added after 1965.

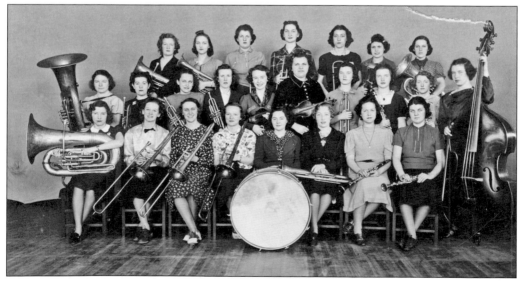

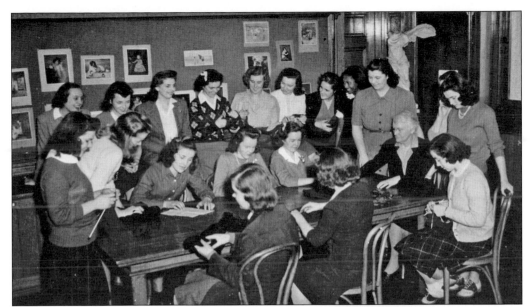

The Art Club drew large numbers. As the 1935 *Knoll* proclaimed: "A little touch of Bohemia, Greenwich Village, and L.T.C. pervades the atmosphere. Smocked creatures rush from all points of the school every Tuesday, take the steps two at a time, dash into the studio, seize their palettes and brushes and work!" The 1943 members pictured here temporarily set aside their palettes to knit scarves and blankets for overseas GIs.

In 1936, Marguerite Gourville arrived as director of physical education, one of Pres. James Dugan's most important hires. Her energy, enthusiasm, and "aversion to languid ladies" resulted in a burst of new activities that endeared her to students; her administrative abilities led to her appointment as dean in 1944 and interim president, between Dugan and O'Leary, in 1950.

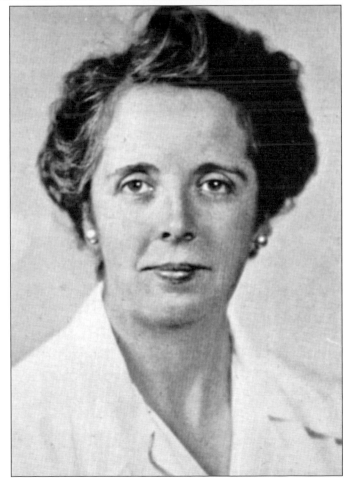

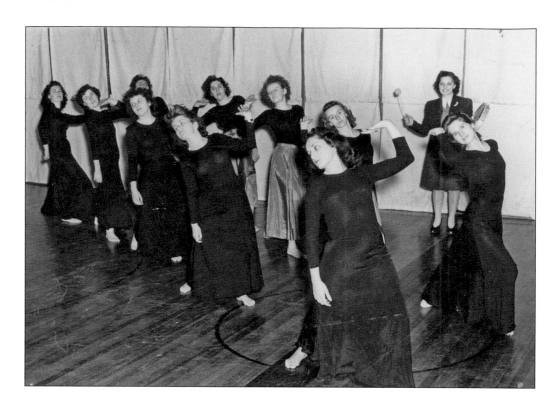

One of Gourville's most popular additions was the modern dance club. Martha Graham had only just mesmerized audiences with her 1936 work *Chronicle*, and Gourville's recognition of the potential of modern dance for college women is a testament to her vision. In the above image, the 1936 club members practice, while the 1938 club poses in the below photograph. The students wrote that "Modern Dance is so called because it grows out of our own environment and expresses our own feelings and time," and they donned black gowns that allowed freedom of movement. Students studied the choreography of Graham, but also created their own dances. The emphasis on rhythmic movement led them to explore Indian dance as well. Gourville helped them organize trips to area performances and invite another founder of American modern dance, Hanya Holm, to campus in 1938.

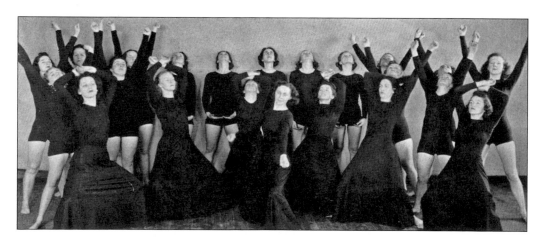

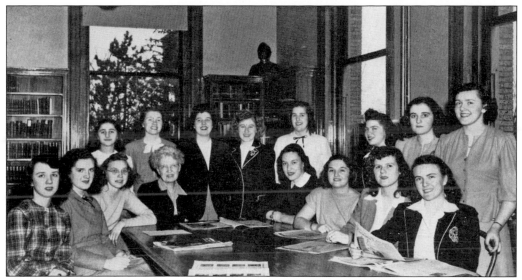

In 1947, students initiated a monthly newspaper called the *Campus Star*. Evelyn Dane, Ruth Hayes, Patricia O'Loughlin, and Angelina Granese served as the first officers, and Christina Kane, who taught English, was their advisor. The paper covered student activities, social events, and any "outside happenings" of educational value and contained cartoons and a good dose of humorous fashion advice. It soon grew in popularity and scope; by 1960, with as many male students involved as female, the staff succinctly summarized the paper's mission: "Its purpose is to inform, educate, entertain, and motivate." Meetings for the paper were held in the Student Activities building, pictured below, a small cottage whose precise location on South Campus remains unknown.

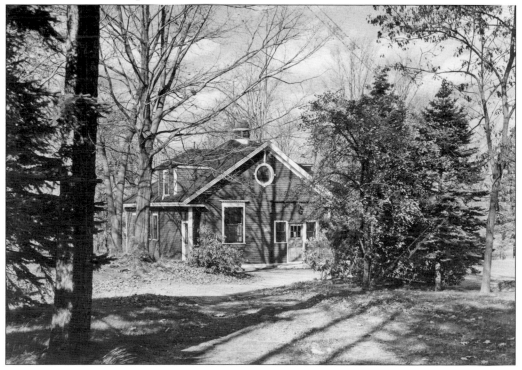

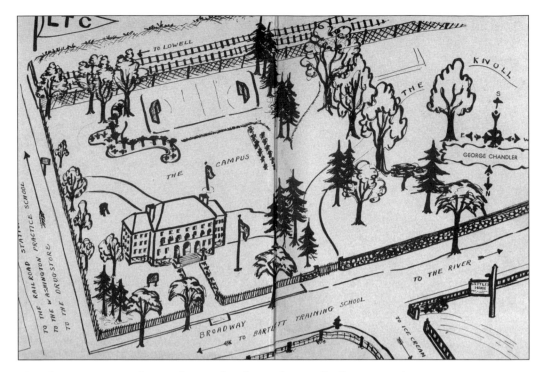

The charming map above, drawn for the 1940 *Knoll*, illustrates the campus amenities, including the area known as "The Knoll" to the right of Coburn Hall. The Butcher family home originally located on the site (and visible in the cover image) was demolished after 1924. The tall evergreens framed panoramic views of the river, and it became such a favorite spot for students that they named the yearbook after it. Tying the name of both the place and the yearbook together, the 1938 staff wrote: "Through this daily living runs a gleam of silver moonlight, the sparkle of snow on the pines, the fresh scent of a grassy hillside—the campus so dear to our hearts held close in memory with two words—The Knoll." The students below sit on "The Knoll" for sketching class. Currently, Mahoney Hall occupies the site.

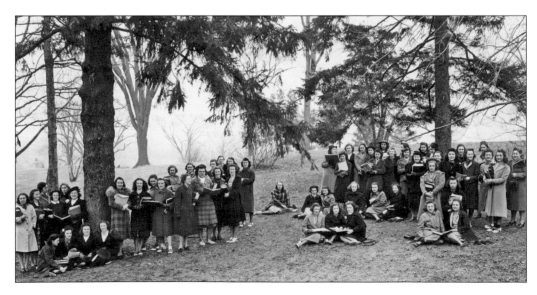

By 1940, the number of male students remained small and the outbreak of World War II meant many of them enlisted. Women continued to organized outings, but the 1943 yearbook authors noted the men's absence: "No longer do the corridors echo with your voices vainly trying to rise above the babble of the more numerous females, but you are not forgotten." The yearbook included pictures of Roger Bell, Sumner Whitestone, James Savas, Fred Hannant, Edward Knowles, Anthony Raisis, Michael Maglio, and John Leganowicz. After the war, the GI Bill had a direct effect on the male/female ratio; as indicated in the image below, men began to swell the ranks of the classes by the late 1940s and early 1950s.

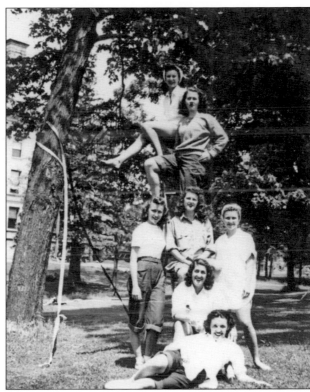

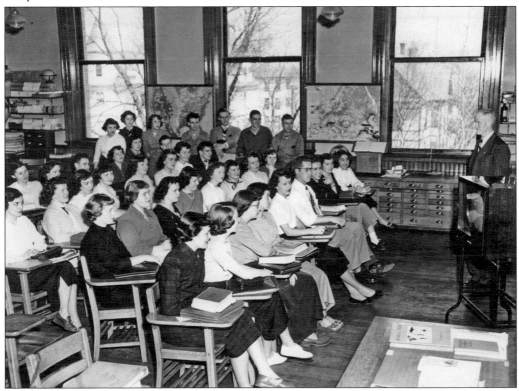

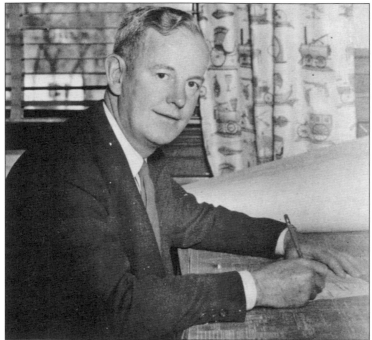

Daniel H. O'Leary succeeded Dugan as president in December 1950. For the next 27 years, O'Leary steered the college through pivotal changes that included the transformation into Lowell State College in 1960 and the merger with Lowell Technological Institute to form the University of Lowell in 1975. During his tenure, O'Leary added new programs, such as nursing, and an entire complex of new buildings.

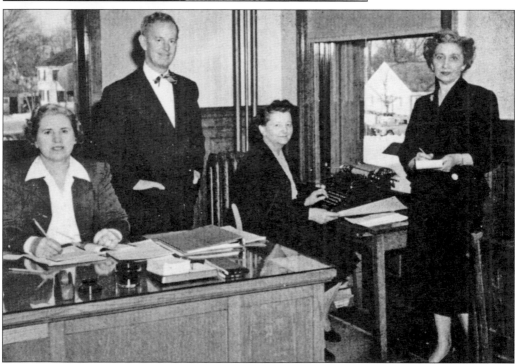

Dugan and O'Leary benefited from the skills of a long-serving and capable staff. Pictured here in 1952 are, from left to right, Kathleen Byrt, Pres. Daniel O'Leary, Florence Braden, and Beatrice Meagher. The administrative offices occupied a suite of rooms on the first floor of Coburn Hall, just to the right of the main entrance (now used as storage and offices for History and Political Science faculty members).

According to Greek mythology, the winged horse Pegasus unleashed the art of poetry when he struck the mount of the muses with his hoof. In 1954, students started an annual literary magazine to showcase fiction, nonfiction, and poetry, dubbing it *Pegasus*. This is the cover of the first *Pegasus*. The completely student-run operation continued into the 1970s.

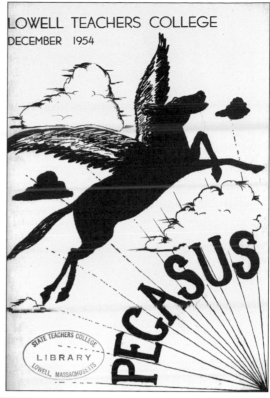

LOWELL TEACHERS COLLEGE
DECEMBER 1954

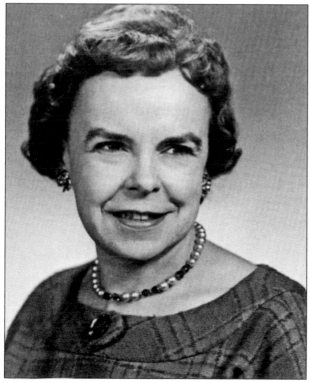

Mary McGauvran graduated from Teachers College in 1939 and, along with a remarkable number of individuals in the institution's history, returned. Hired in 1952, she had a long and influential career. McGauvran served as director of admissions, assistant dean of women, and director of student affairs; she taught courses on campus and in the graduate program at Boston University and earned a national reputation for her work in assessment and testing.

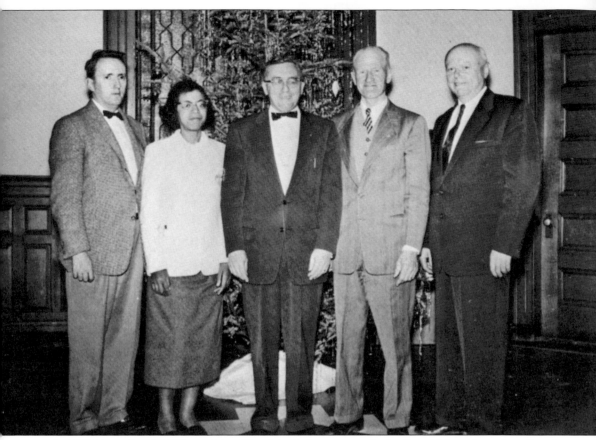

In 1957, Pres. Daniel O'Leary hired Patricia Goler—not only the first African American female faculty member with a PhD, but also the first African American woman with a PhD in the state college system. Goler, shown here in 1959 with Social Sciences department colleagues, from left to right, Frederick Norton, Francis O'Hara, Edward Knowles, and John Fitzgerald, later served as chairperson of the history department and in 1975 as the Liberal Arts dean. The university's Goler Fellows Program is named in her honor.

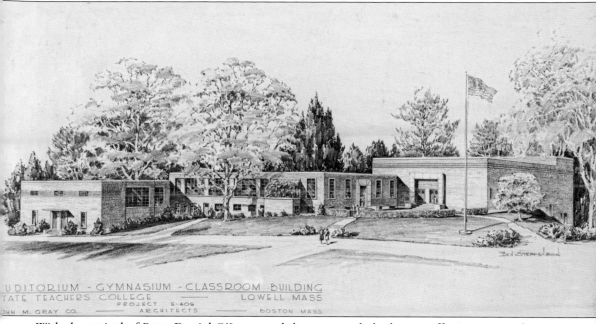

UDITORIUM - GYMNASIUM - CLASSROOM BUILDING
TATE TEACHERS COLLEGE — LOWELL MASS
PROJECT 5·406
JHN M. GRAY CO. — ARCHITECTS — BOSTON MASS

With the arrival of Pres. Daniel O'Leary and the postwar baby boom, efforts were made to expand the college. The knoll next to Coburn, so popular with the students, was chosen as the site for a building that contained a gymnasium, auditorium, and classrooms. The architect, John M. Gray of Boston, provided a stripped modernist design typical in the mid-1950s. The building was later named for John Mahoney, the school's second principal.

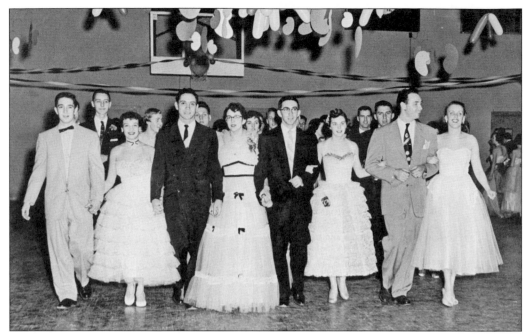

The new building was immediately put to use. The dances once held in Coburn Hall's assembly room were now held in the gymnasium; similarly, annual commencement exercises moved from Coburn to the new auditorium. The annual "Artists Ball" used strategically placed balloons and Calderesque mobiles to obscure backboards and buzzer clocks. The Men's Athletic Association, a relatively new and growing club, used the gym for a variety of sporting activities, including basketball, volleyball, badminton, and a lifesaving course. Basketball attained varsity status by 1957; below, an LTC player loses the opening tip-off to rival Salem State in a home game. At Coburn, the assembly room was converted into much-needed library space.

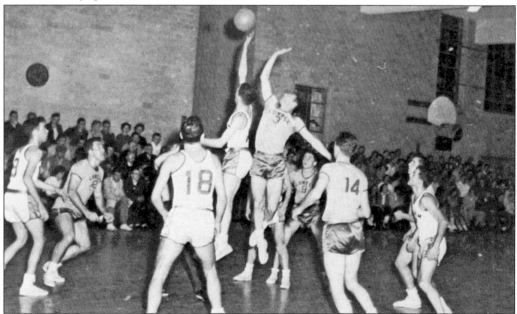

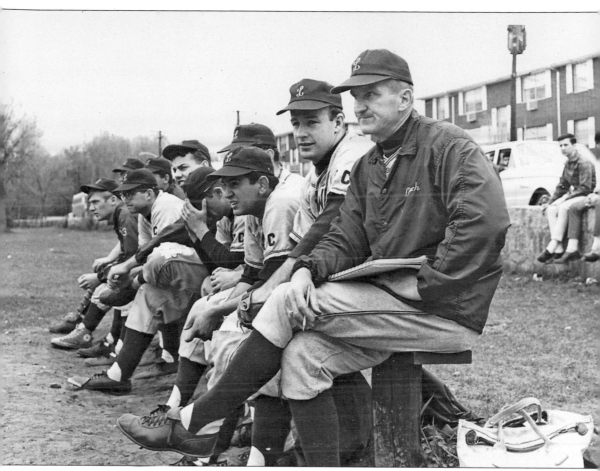

Ignatius James Ciszek mentored the college's athletic successes. He arrived as coordinator of athletics in 1953 and helped establish the men's basketball and baseball programs. In 1957, only four years after he started the baseball program, the team won the New England Teachers College Athletic Conference Championship. Following the 1975 merger, Ciszek became athletic director and remained in that position until his retirement in 1986.

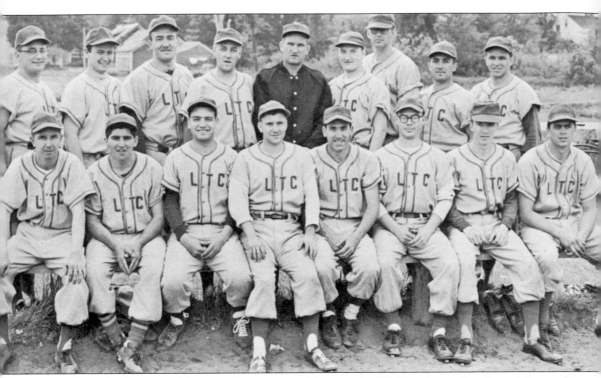

Without doubt, one of the most important athletes under I.J. Ciszek was Leo Parent (second row, third from left). A star in both basketball and baseball, he helped both teams earn acclaim. In 1957, Parent was voted Most Outstanding Performer in Small College Baseball and is shown here with the 1958 LTC baseball team. His sensational ability led the New York Yankees to bring him into their farm system for five years.

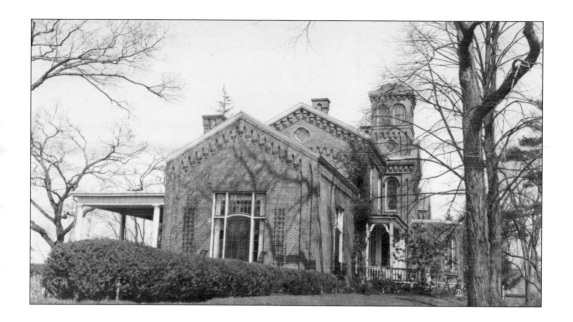

O'Leary continued to expand the college's physical size—Dugan Hall followed Mahoney, and in 1957, the college acquired Allen House for use as a dormitory, shown above and below. The oldest structure on South Campus, it has served many uses. Abiel Rolfe built the house in 1854; in 1890, Charles Allen purchased it and named it "Terraces" because of the paved and lawn terraces that offered sweeping views up the Merrimack River. Allen, who helped to site Coburn Hall, achieved national prominence. His illustrious career in state politics was crowned by a series of appointments made by President McKinley—first as assistant secretary of the Navy and then as the first civilian governor of Puerto Rico. Allen was also an amateur painter; he added a music room and art gallery to the house.

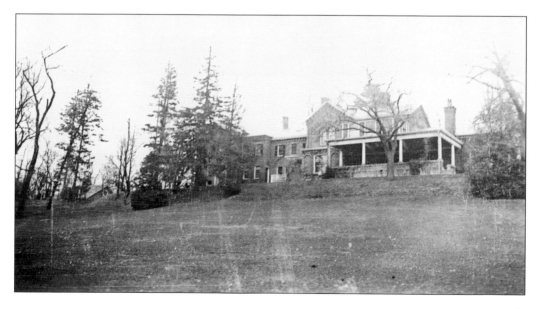

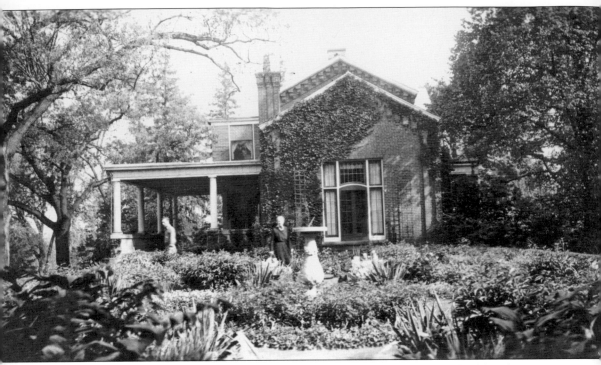

This view highlights the Italianate detailing of the house: the corbelled brick cornices, asymmetry, and quatrefoil windows are typical characteristics of a style popularized in the mid-1850s by architects like A.J. Downing. Key to Downing's vision was the integration of house and landscape, as evidenced by the house's lush garden.

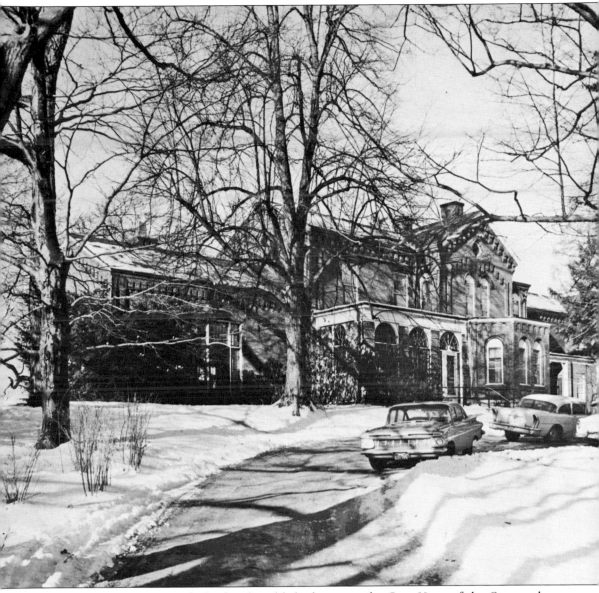

After Allen's death in 1934, the family sold the house to the Grey Nuns of the Cross, who sold it to President O'Leary. First used as a dormitory and then as office and classroom space through the mid-1970s, its physical condition deteriorated. The university recently completed a $1.5-million renovation, and it now serves as the chancellor's office. The building is listed in the National Register of Historic Places.

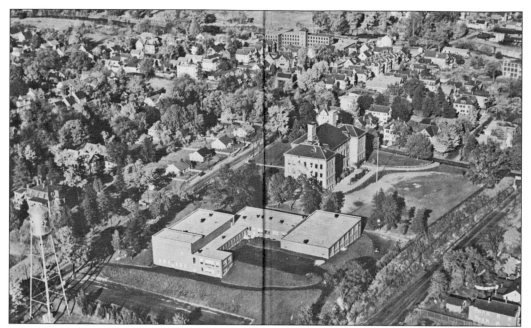

Pres. Daniel O'Leary's building fever did not stop. All through the 1960s, he worked unceasingly to create an entire complex of buildings that would define the campus. As these above (1959) and below (1975) aerials suggest, his effort forever changed the character of the area. Twenty-six acres of the residential neighborhood opposite Coburn Hall were acquired and leveled. Because it served as a dormitory, Allen House was allowed to remain. The complex included a new science building, a student activities building, a library, a cafeteria, and a music building, among others. The architects, Vincent Solomita and Joseph Palermo, provided a design in the fashionable Brutalist style (popular on college campuses), the hallmarks of which included a preponderance of concrete and sharp, clean geometric forms. Despite numerous delays, the primary buildings were completed by the mid-1970s.

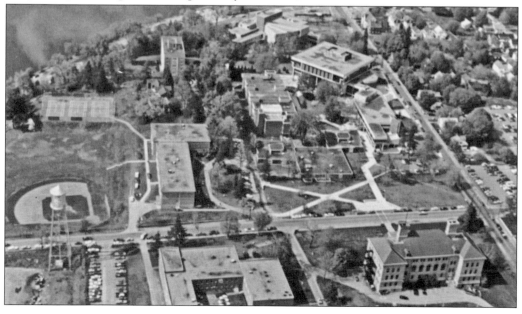

Four

BEYOND TEXTILES

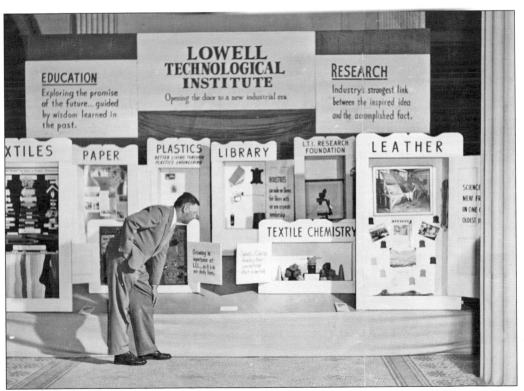

The textile-driven curriculum of the Lowell Textile Institute underwent a fundamental change at mid-century, as attested by the school's contribution to the 1954 Industrial Exhibit at the Massachusetts State House. Each poster represented a new endeavor at the institute, showcasing efforts to diversify the curriculum by addressing numerous needs in Massachusetts industry. To reinforce this expansion, the institute changed its name from Lowell Textile Institute to Lowell Technological Institute in 1955.

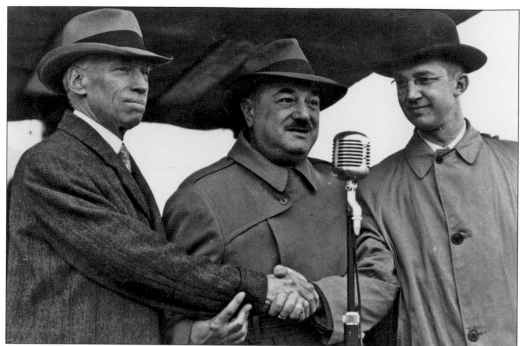

The shift in the institute's direction came with a shift in leadership. When Charles Eames retired in 1945, he was replaced by 29-year-old Kenneth Fox (class of 1938). Fox immediately began to expand both academic programs and the physical structure of the institute. Shown above with Eames (left) and Samuel Pinanski (center), chairman of the board of trustees, Fox oversaw the laying of the cornerstone of Smith Hall (a dormitory) in 1947, part of a new complex of buildings (pictured below). The number of students at the institute shrunk dramatically during World War II—down to a senior class of 12 in 1945—but burgeoned just as dramatically following the passage of the GI Bill. The freshman class of 1946 had 175 students, the vast majority of whom were veterans. Fox's first response was to enlarge the campus with new dormitories and a library.

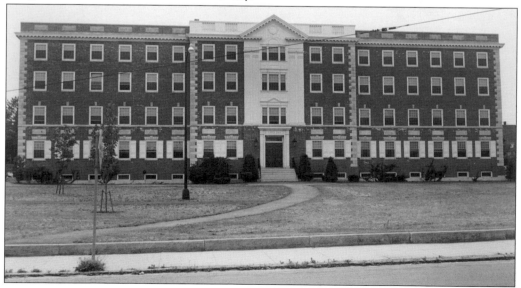

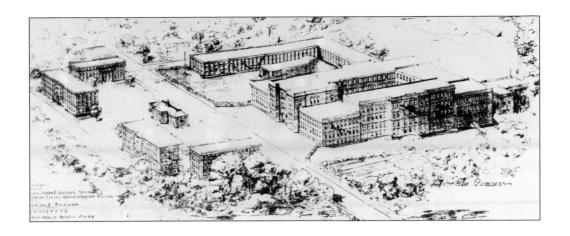

The above aerial architectural rendering from 1949 shows Kenneth Fox's initial plan for four dorms arranged around a central library located on a plot across from Southwick, with another complex of buildings adjacent to Southwick. The plan went through a series of revisions and only two of the four dorms, Smith and Eames, were built. The 1953 aerial photograph below shows the results. Instead of putting the library or dorms on axis with Southwick, the architects, Krokyn and Browne of Boston, established a new axis that unified the expansion. The library and dorms are centered to face the entire block occupied by Southwick (between the highway and Riverside Street), allowing Southwick and the new buildings to act together as one balancing entity; this was a small but effective piece of campus planning.

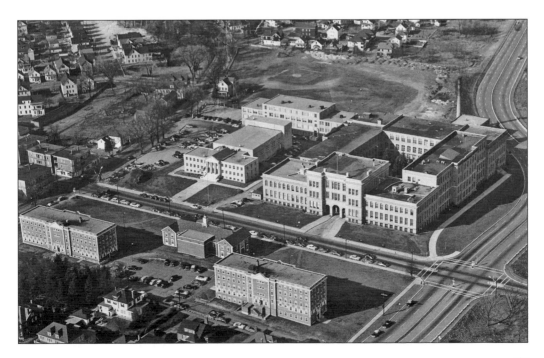

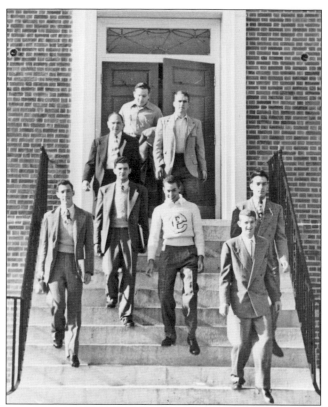

The new dormitories, Smith and Eames, were quickly filled with an influx of postwar students. Many of the rooms were doubles, and amenities included a cafeteria and open study and lounge areas. The below image depicts the much-frequented cafeteria in the basement of Smith. Although the student body was still primarily male, female students frequented the public spaces, especially in 1954. That year, a serious fire in Coburn Hall at the Teachers College across the river closed the building. In response, LTI offered the use of classroom space in Southwick so that Teachers College students could complete their studies; the proximity of the study and lounge areas in Smith and Eames (just opposite Southwick) made them a popular between-classes haven.

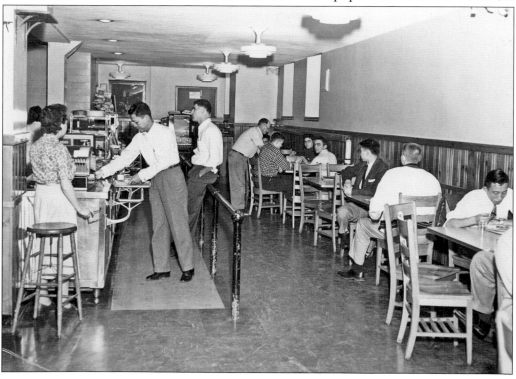

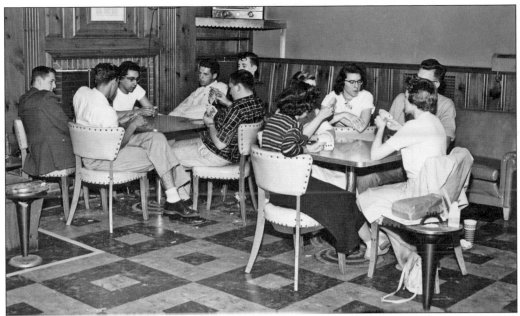

The residents of Eames cheerfully welcomed the Teachers College students, writing in the *Pickout* that the women's presence made more than a few of the men improve their appearances. Shown above is the lounge area in Eames, which was often used by the bridge club. The new Alumni Memorial Library (below), flanked by the dormitories, served as the anchor of the complex. Architects Krokyn and Browne provided an elegant example of Georgian Colonial Revival architecture. The red brick and white trim underscore its pleasing classical proportions, and the high, round-arched windows with prominent keystones allowed natural light to flood the main reading area. Changes to the building, such as the removal of the front entrance and the addition of Lydon Library in 1970 at the rear, have diminished but not overridden its essential qualities.

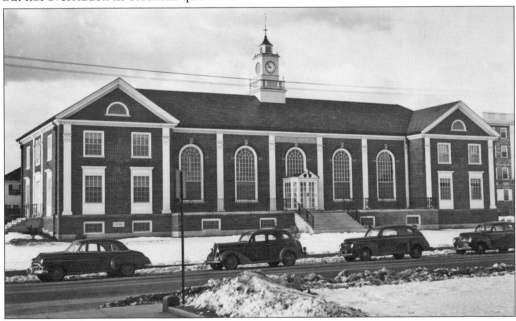

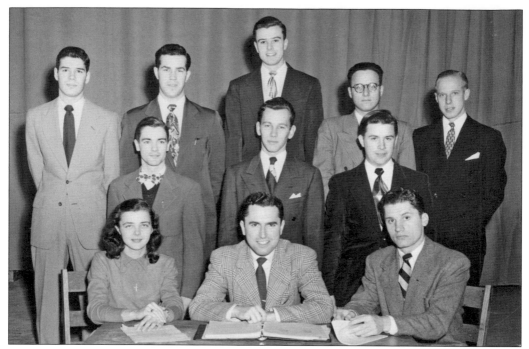

It was also under Kenneth Fox's administration that students put together an effective student government association, with officers elected annually; as the officers stated in the 1949 *Pickout*, "In March of 1948, the dream of a functional Student Council at L.T.I. finally became a reality." After a "spirited" contest, Irwin Smoler won the presidency, with David Pfister and Robert Sloan as vice president and treasurer, respectively. The association regularly met with the administration to address issues of concern, such as the need for more dormitories—an issue on which the association and Fox saw eye to eye. The below image depicts the 1949 election, and the successful candidates are shown above.

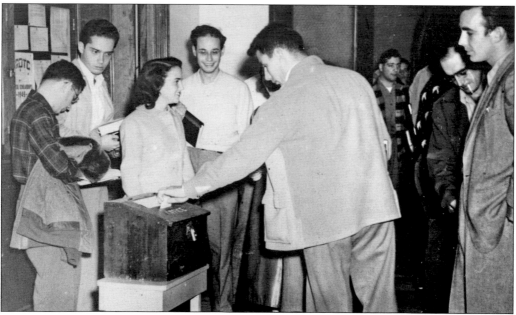

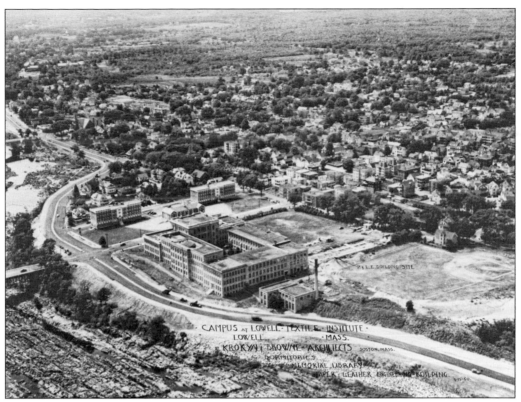

As part of an effort to develop non-textile programs, Kenneth Fox pushed for research in other industries, such as paper and leather, and allocated funds for a new building with laboratories. Krokyn and Browne also designed this building, pictured below, but instead of repeating the classical idiom of the library, they employed a restrained Art Deco modern style. Later additions have obscured the nicely designed entrances shown in the architects' rendering of the building. The 1952 aerial photograph above indicates the foundation work for the new Paper and Leather Engineering Building, set at a 90-degree angle to Kitson. Cumnock was yet to be built, and Falmouth Street has all but disappeared. When the leather program dissolved and the paper program became part of chemical engineering, the building was renamed the Engineering Building.

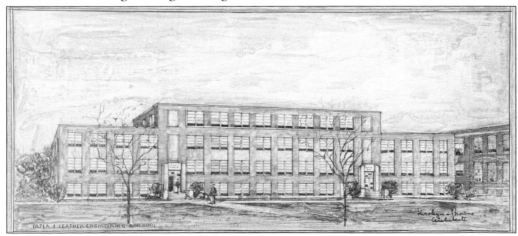

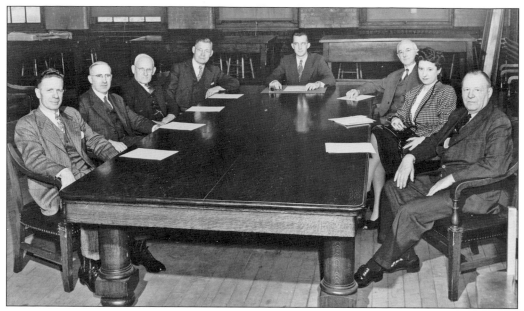

In September of his first term, Kenneth Fox called a meeting with the faculty. Conspicuous among them was Vittoria Rosatto, the only full-time female faculty member at LTI. She was a member of the fabric design department (which she subsequently chaired) but remained in the minority; LTI did not hire additional female faculty members until the mid-1960s. At the table with Rosatto and Fox was the long-serving Gilbert Merrill (second from left). Head of the cotton yarn department, and equally liked and esteemed by students and colleagues, he coauthored the standard textbook for the industry, *American Cotton Handbook*, in 1941. The below 1950s image of the knitting laboratory shows how extensive the apparati had become. Prof. Nathaniel Jones stands at the back (with hand on hip) and Prof. Albert Woidzik, in the left foreground, sports a bow tie.

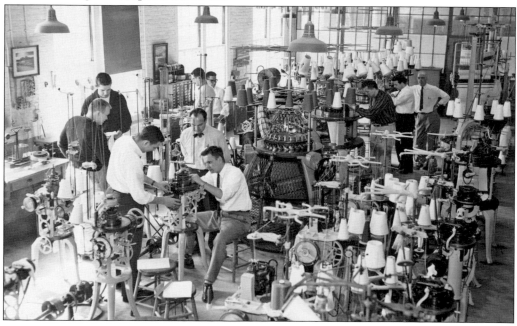

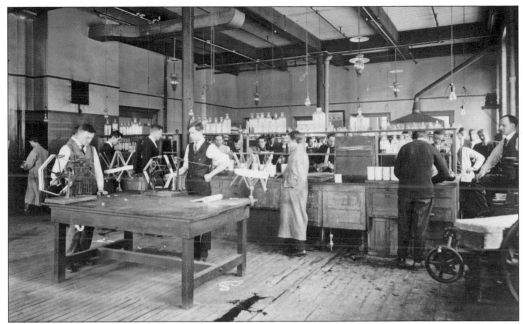

The legacy of Louis Atwell Olney lived on in the textile chemistry department. The undated image above depicts the old dye lab in Southwick, located just behind the large lecture room. Beakers, used to mix colors, are plentiful, and a hooded exhaust at the rear drew fumes out of the room. Students at left are winding yarn for dyeing. The professor at far right against the window is most likely Robert Sleeper. As technology changed, so did classrooms. In the below image of a later dye lab, an unidentified individual works with a pressure dying machine. A cake of yarn has been inserted into the pot—similar to a pressure cooker—for a fast infusion of color through the entire fiber.

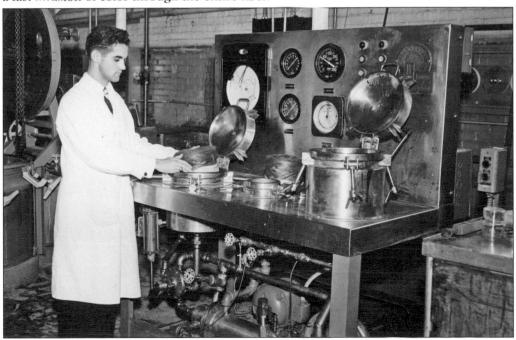

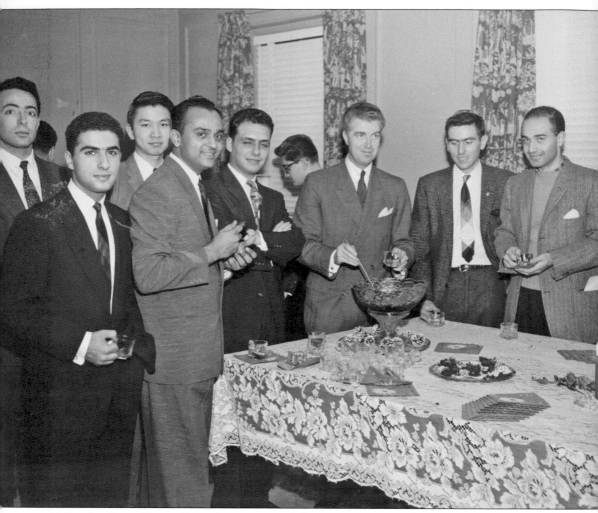

Following Pres. Kenneth Fox's unexpected departure in 1950, the board of trustees again picked a young and dynamic successor, Martin J. Lydon (third from right), who had served as dean of students. Working closely with Everett Olsen, Lydon continued Fox's mission of enlarging the academic programs and physical space of LTI. Lydon's political and social connections won legislative support, but his popularity with faculty and students ebbed and flowed. He retired in 1972.

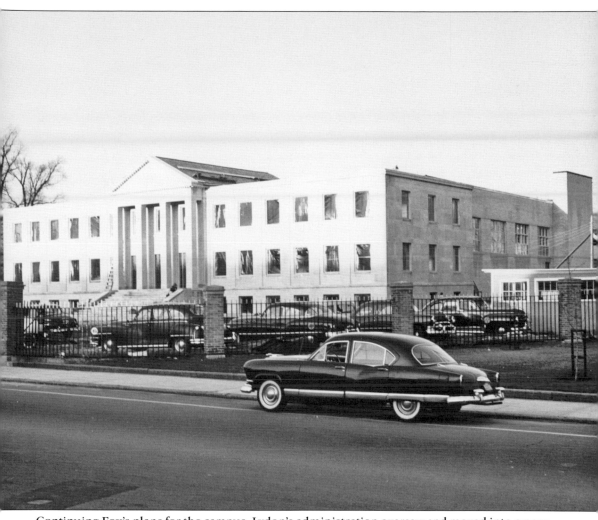

Continuing Fox's plans for the campus, Lydon's administration oversaw and moved into a new administration building—Cumnock Hall. Constructed next to Southwick, it completed architects Krokyn and Browne's original plan for the campus. The building was named for Alexander Cumnock, the first chairman of the board of trustees. The back of the building contained a large auditorium, which was put to immediate and regular use by the Textile Players.

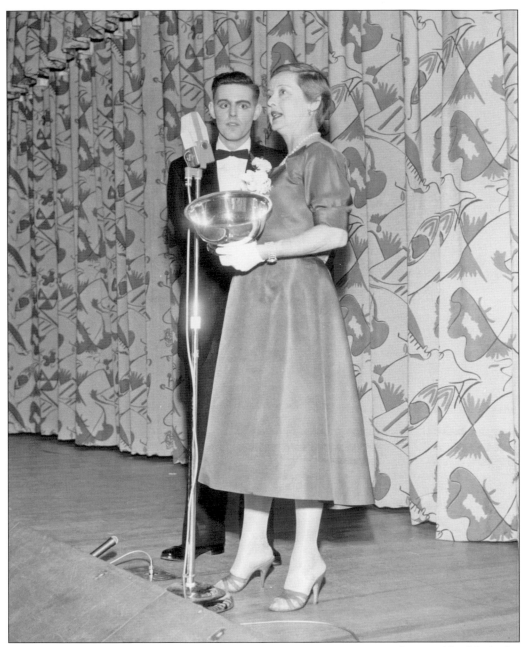

The timing of the new auditorium could not have been better. An undisputed highlight for students in 1956 was a visit by Lowell native Bette Davis. Davis had already made her mark in Hollywood with *Jezebel* (1938) and her golden decade of performances in the 1940s. She is pictured with Frederick Obear, a member of the Textile Players, on stage in front of a sold-out audience.

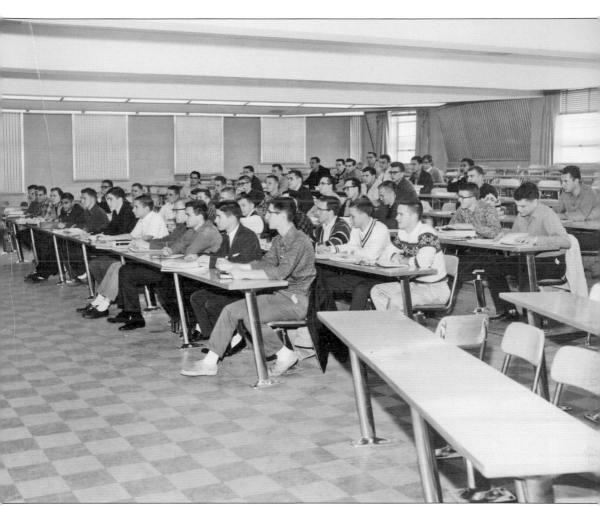

Open space on campus continued to spark speculation. The site next to Cumnock, along Riverside Street, was tagged for a new Industrial Research Building. Completed in 1964 after an extended construction period, it is now known as Ball Hall in honor of mechanical engineer Herbert Ball. This image depicts Room 210, which is still in use today but now has a layer of carpet over the linoleum, along with other upgrades.

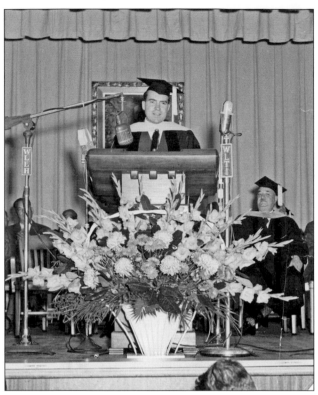

Under Martin Lydon, LTI offered a growing number of honorary degrees to nationally and internationally recognized scholars and politicians. In 1954, LTI bestowed a degree on Richard M. Nixon, then vice president under Dwight D. Eisenhower. In 1958, Sen. John F. Kennedy (shown below walking out of the recently finished Cumnock Hall) received an honorary degree. The subsequent history of these two men had its own impact on students. When Kennedy was assassinated, students included a memorial page for him in the yearbook. Nixon fared far differently—the student council voted to rescind his degree in 1972, a full two years before Nixon's resignation from office in 1974.

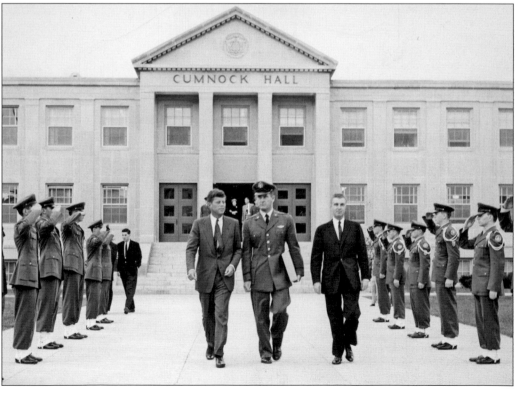

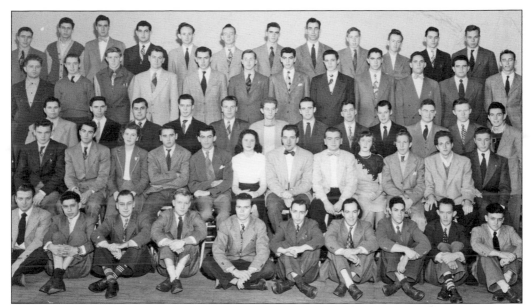

Despite the postwar growth in enrollment, the percentage of female students remained as low as before the war. The graduating class of 1951, pictured above, contained just three women. Many still majored in textile and fabric design, with only a few choosing chemistry or engineering programs. Efforts to draw top-performing high school students in the 1960s included a series of scholarships. Natalie Wojick, pictured below at right, won a scholarship in plastics technology in 1964. The plastics engineering program, founded in 1954, gained prominence in the 1960s under the able direction of professors Russell Ehlers, Henry Thomas, and Raymond Normandin. Wojick also served as historian for Phi Sigma Rho, the only sorority on campus.

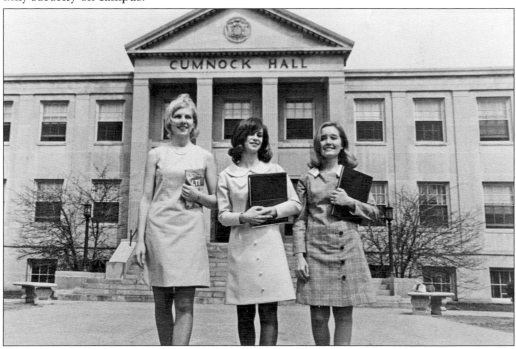

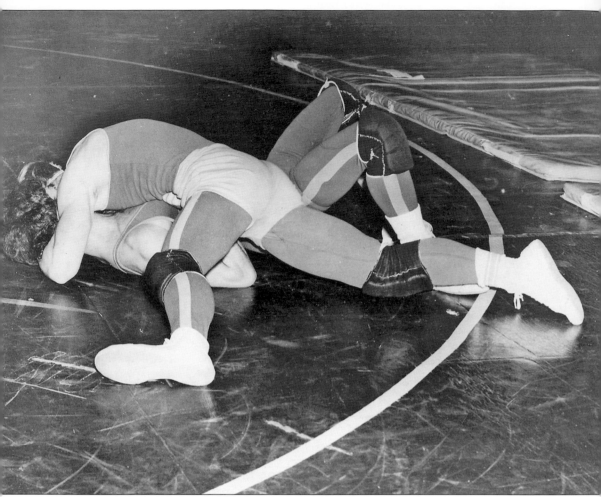

LTI built a new, long-overdue gymnasium in 1967 to replace the fourth-floor gymnasium in Southwick (in use since 1903), naming it for Lowellian Thomas F. Costello. In the 1960s, LTI added new varsity sports such as golf (1964), wrestling (1965), cross-country (1966), tennis (1971), and men's soccer (1972). In this mid-1960s photograph, star wrestler Bob Germann (top) outmaneuvers an opponent.

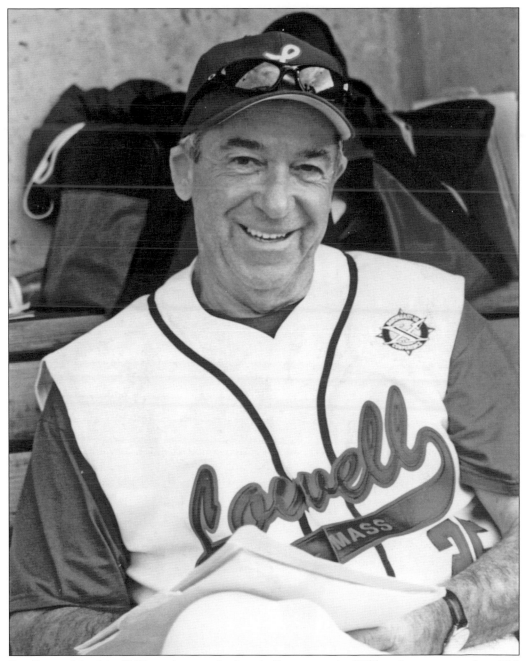

Jim Stone, hired in 1965, took over the baseball program in 1966 and won more than 800 games in 37 years. After falling short in 12 previous NCAA tournament bids, the team won consecutive NCAA Northeast Region crowns and trips to the Division II College World Series in 2001 and 2002. (Courtesy of UMass Lowell Athletics Department.)

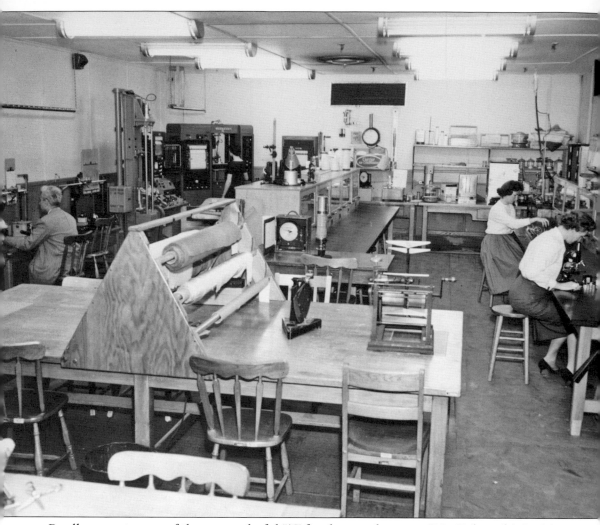

By all accounts, one of the most colorful LTI faculty members was Fritz Kobayashi. In this 1950s image, he is on the left at the single yarn tester in the textile testing lab, located in Pasteur Hall. At the end of each spring term, he would "ship out" and spend the summer steaming along the coast of South America.

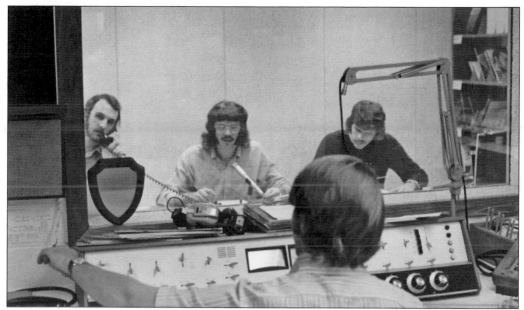

Students have long been proud of the campus radio station. Started in the basement of Eames Hall after World War II, it broadcast as WLTI-AM and went on-air at 7:00 p.m. The student-run station's primary purpose, as stated in the *Pickout*, was "to bring to the student body, living in the dormitories, the type of music they want when they want it." The station could only be heard on campus. In 1963, the station upgraded to FM. Now known as WUML 91.5, the station continues to bring diverse programming to the community with 24-hour broadcasts of music as well as commentary and comedy. Students still run the station, although community DJs get the mike from 9:00 a.m. until noon. In the image below, Bob Naylor (class of 2010) broadcasts from the station's home in Lydon Library. (Below, courtesy of Steve Moffatt.)

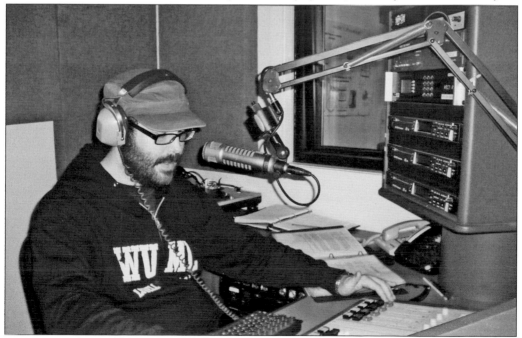

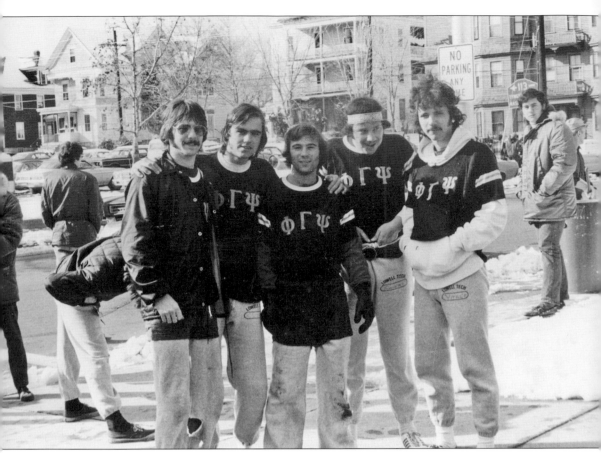

Fraternities have a long history at the institution. Three textile fraternities were established within the first six years of opening—Delta Kappa Phi (in 1900), Omicron Pi (in 1902), and Phi Psi (in 1903). They flourished in size and number and many eventually occupied large houses in the neighborhood around LTI. After a hiatus, they have once again become active members of campus life.

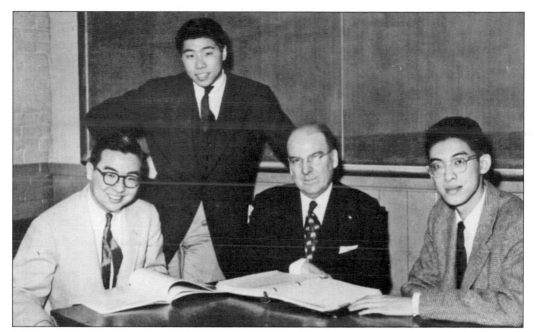

Minorities at the institute often formed their own clubs. The Chinese Students Circle, pictured above in 1955 with advisor professor James Dow, claimed to be the oldest student club, with a founding date in the late 1920s. Indian students formed an association in 1957, the Latin American Society began in 1962 (members of the club are pictured below in the early 1970s), and the African American Society formed in 1967. Each club fostered friendships and helped give minorities a united voice. The Latin American Society organized events to introduce the student body to the music, films, and food of Latin America. The African American Society pushed the university to hire an affirmative action officer.

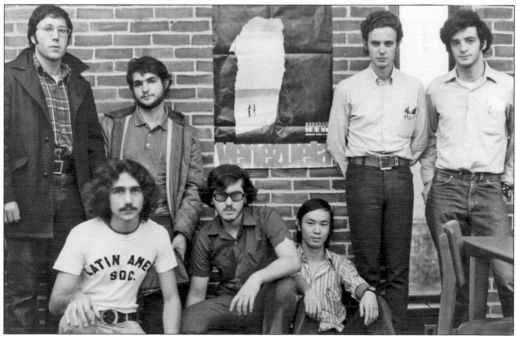

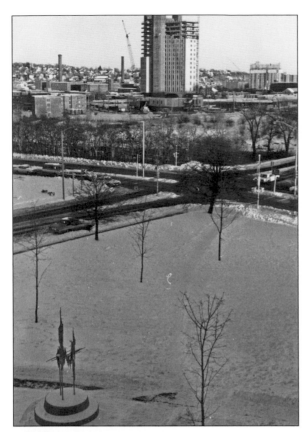

In 1973, construction began on a high-rise dormitory now known as Fox Hall. It sat at an angle from the Leitch and Bourgois dormitories built in the mid-1960s. Fox Hall is seen above from a window in Smith Hall. The aerial photograph below gives a good indication of the context. This entire site (now called East Campus) was once part of the densely populated Franco American neighborhood known as Little Canada. The neighborhood was bulldozed in the early 1960s as part of Lowell's nascent urban renewal program. By acquiring this land, LTI extended its presence across the Merrimack River and closer to downtown Lowell.

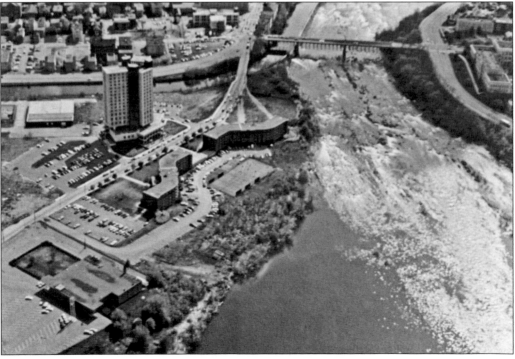

Five

FORGING MERGERS

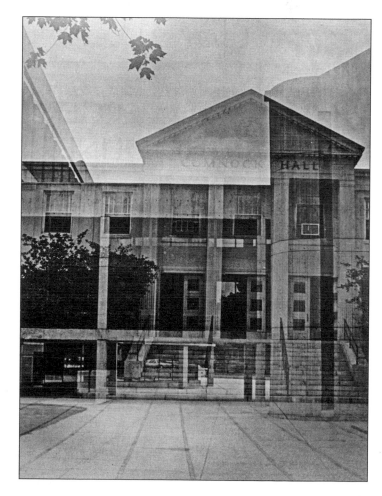

By the early 1970s, both Lowell State College and Lowell Technological Institute had grown in numbers of students, programs and degrees and sheer physical size. After a series of committees, commissions, and surveys addressed the idea of a merger, the University of Lowell came into being in 1975. Everett Olsen was named acting president and Daniel O'Leary was named chancellor while a national search was conducted for a new president.

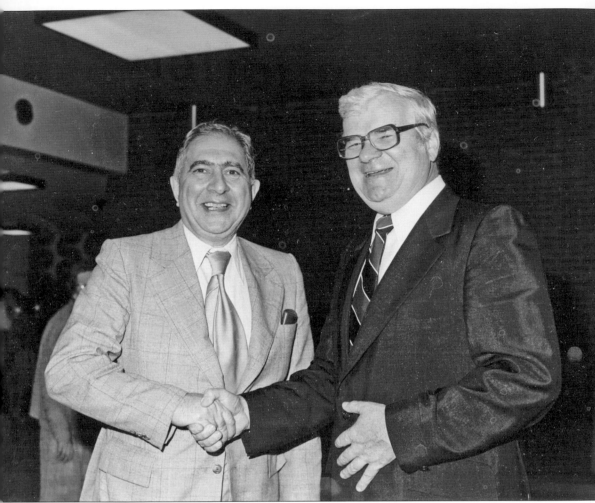

John B. Duff was named the first president of the University of Lowell in 1976. He restructured the administration and fostered the growth of new initiatives, such as the continuing education program. One of the most important new directions he gave to the university's mission, however, was a renewed integration with the Lowell community. Duff (right) is shown here with Prof. Leon Beghian (left).

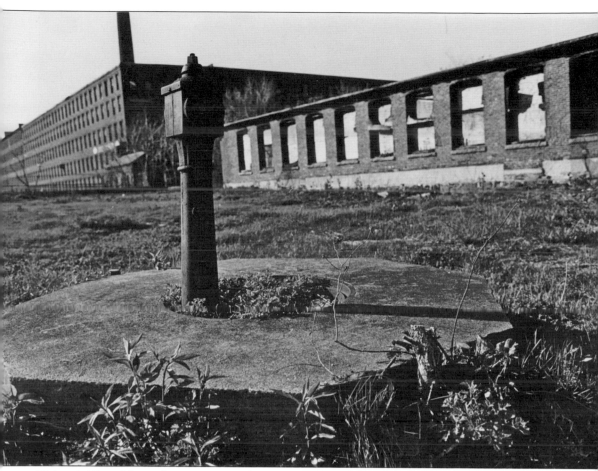

Richard Allen (class of 1979) emerged as one student receptive to Duff's attempts to build connections with the city. Allen served as editor of the yearbook in 1979, and unique amidst a long series of yearbooks, Allen included numerous photographs of the city, like this one, to connect his university experience with the mills that had prompted the college's founding over 80 years earlier.

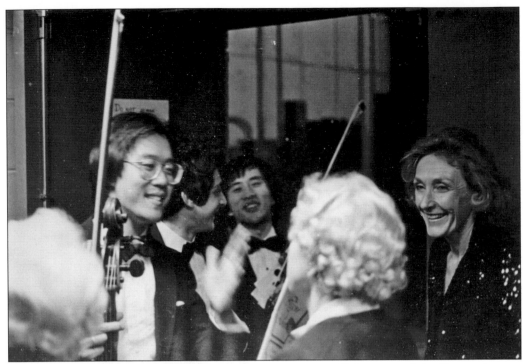

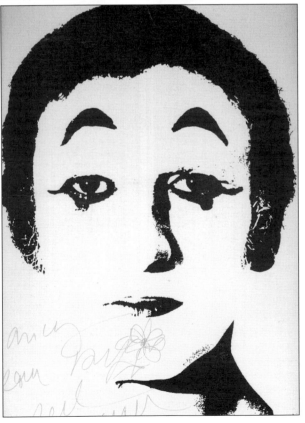

Duff also started the University of Lowell Foundation, whose members worked energetically to enhance the city's cultural offerings. In the late 1970s and early 1980s, events included performances by cellist Yo-Yo Ma (at left in the above image), violinist Isaac Stern, and the famous mime Marcel Marceau (left). In the 1990s, the celebrity series evolved into the Center for the Arts, which also offered a children's performing arts enrichment program that at one time served 50,000 school children annually. Today's UMass Lowell Center for Arts and Ideas produces and promotes cultural affairs activities on campus and in downtown Lowell. (Both, courtesy of Nancy Donohue.)

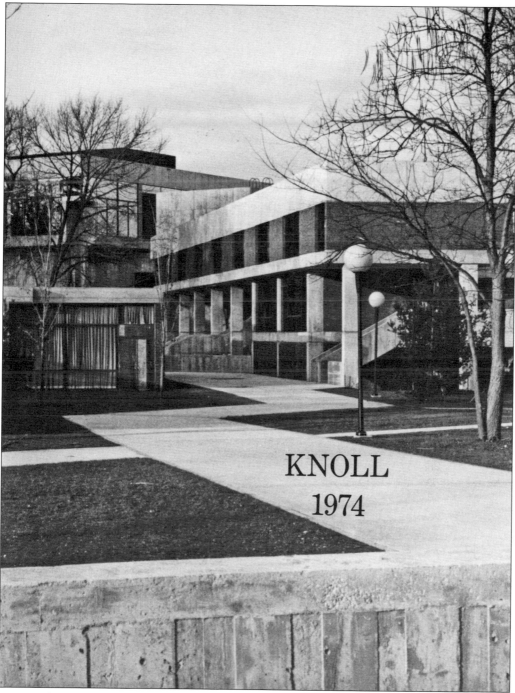

KNOLL
1974

On South Campus, the completion of the quad buildings was tied into the merger. This image from the 1974 *Knoll* gives a good indication of what the newly finished complex looked like, with the clean geometric lines of its walkways and modernist globe lighting. A key feature of the Brutalist style was the absence of decoration or ornament so that materials were appreciated for themselves (hence the unpolished concrete wall in the foreground that reveals the wooden formwork that held it while it cured).

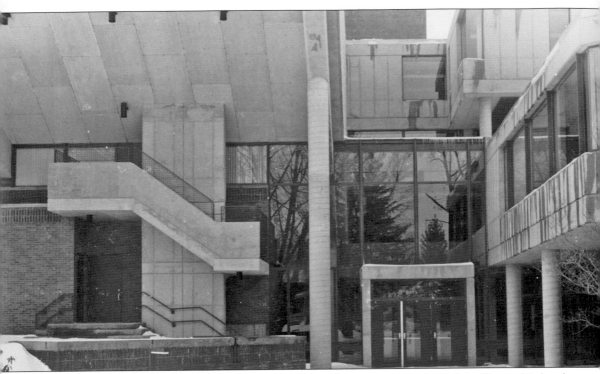

The music building was named for Cyrus Durgin, the second principal of the Normal School. It includes a 1,000-seat concert hall and opened in 1976 with great fanfare and a performance of Puccini's *La Boheme*. Currently, it also serves as the offices of the Dean of the College of Fine Arts, Humanities, and Social Sciences.

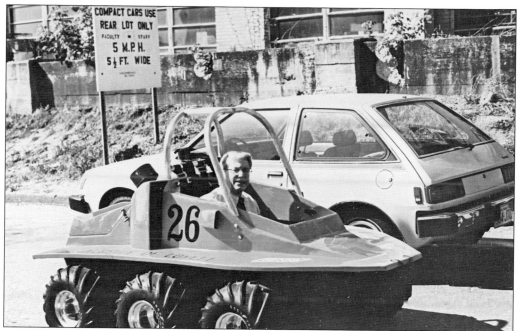

On North Campus, Aldo Crugnola stepped into the driver's seat as the dean of the College of Engineering in 1977 and remained there until 1996. The college included the accredited departments of chemical, civil, electrical, mechanical, nuclear, and plastics engineering. In the mid-1980s, the college itself was named for famed 19th-century engineer (and Lowell native) James B. Francis, whose innovations in efficient turbines are still used today. (Courtesy of Aldo Crugnola.)

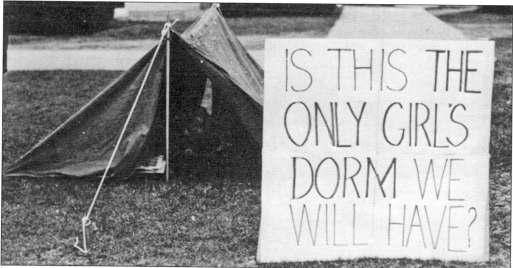

While the administration worked to improve academic programs, female students protested for more housing in 1970. Concordia Hall dormitory was built on South Campus in 1966 but largely reserved for music students. On North Campus, the Smith and Eames dormitories were dedicated for male students. On East Campus, the rooms in Leitch and Bourgois were quickly filled. The addition of Fox Hall helped, as did the construction of Sheehy and Donohue dormitories in 1989.

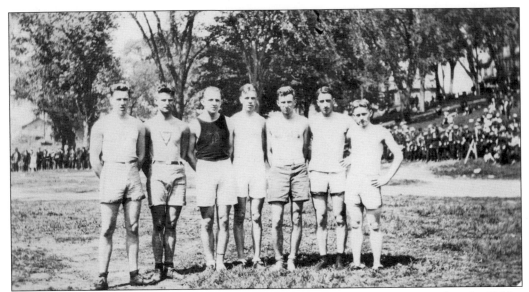

The merger also greatly benefitted the athletic program. In the 1970s and early 1980s, University of Lowell teams from a variety of sports gained national recognition. A track team banded together in 1902, and its success was boosted by the inclusion of a cinder track around the playing fields outside of Kitson. The above image shows the 1920s track team. The team received its greatest boost decades later, in 1970, when George Davis (pictured below, at right) arrived at LTI as the coach of cross-country and track and field—a program that had just received varsity status in 1966. Within years, Davis's teams brought four NCAA titles to the institution. In 1991, the men's cross-country team reached the pinnacle of competition when it captured the NCAA Division II title. (Below, courtesy of UMass Lowell Athletics Department.)

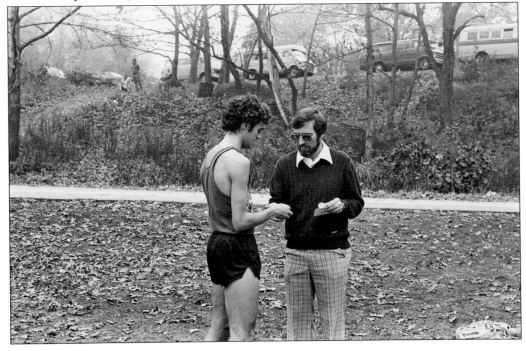

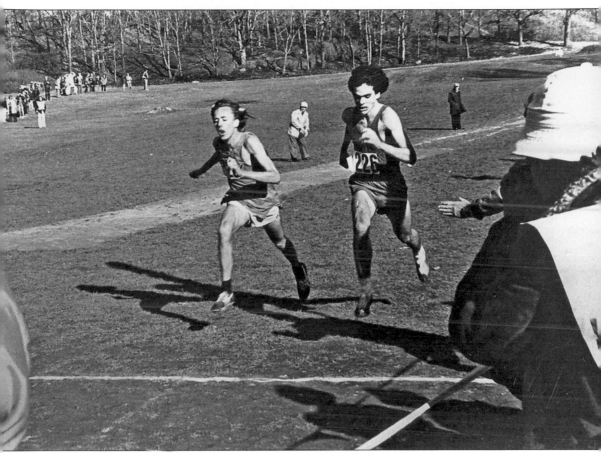

One of the outstanding athletes of Davis's team was track star Vin Fleming. Just months after the 1975 merger, the University of Lowell's first national champion was crowned after a dramatic finish. Fleming (right) passed leader Joel Jameson on the final step to win the 1975 NCAA Division III Cross Country Championship. (Courtesy of UMass Lowell Athletics Department.)

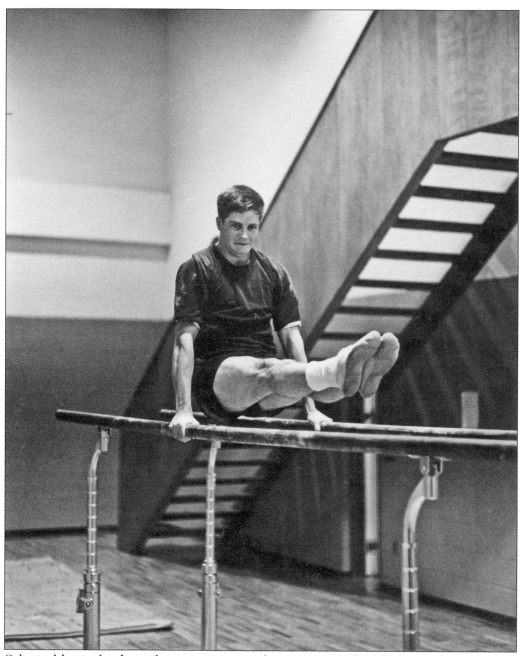

Other athletes also brought recognition to the University of Lowell. Gymnastics gained momentum in the late 1960s, as demonstrated by the unidentified student pictured. John Albhergini, a standout gymnast, won the NCAA Division II crown on the parallel bars in 1979. In track and field, Mark Linscheid claimed championships in the hammer throw in the NCAA Division III competition of 1977 and again in Division II in 1980.

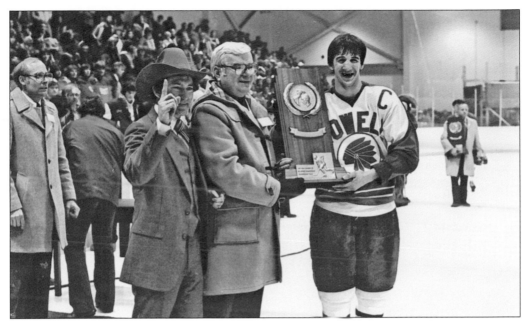

Bill Riley took over the hockey program in 1969 and went on to win three NCAA Division II Championships—in 1979, 1981, and 1982. These wins spearheaded the university's transition into Division I and Hockey East, the premier division of collegiate hockey. Riley (left, in hat) is pictured after the 1981 championship game with Pres. John Duff (center) and All American captain Dean Jenkins (right). (Courtesy of UMass Lowell Athletics Department.)

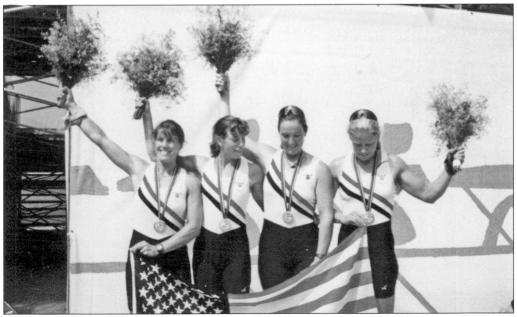

Shelagh Donohoe (left) found her vocation the minute she stepped into a shell and rowed onto the Merrimack River. A standout undergraduate rower in the mid-1980s, Donohoe led UMass Lowell to a bronze medal in the prestigious Dad Vail Regatta in Philadelphia in 1987. She went on to win a silver medal in the 1992 Barcelona Olympics. She now coaches at the University of Rhode Island. (Courtesy of UMass Lowell Athletics Department.)

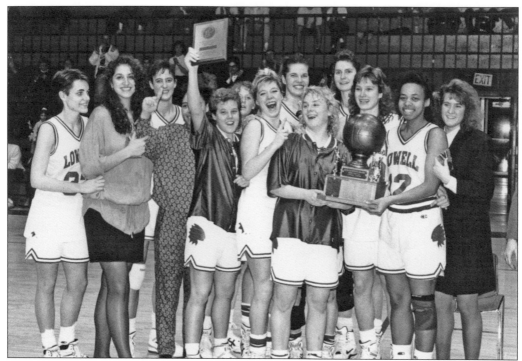

By 1973, there were two varsity sports available to the women at State College: basketball and volleyball. The push to enhance women's sports, especially after the merger, came from physical education professors Denise Legault and Claire Chamberlain. The basketball team won the New England Collegiate Conference six times in the 1990s, and the volleyball team won the Northeast-10 championship in 2009. Pictured above is the 1990–1991 team. Pictured below is the 2009 volleyball team. (Courtesy of UMass Lowell Athletics Department.)

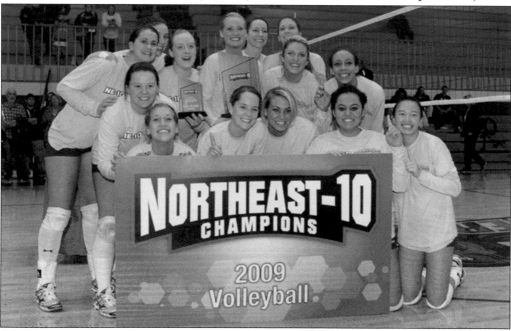

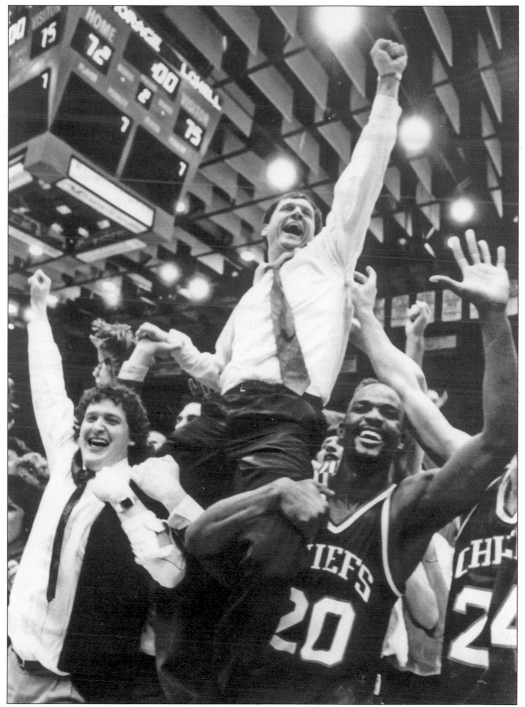

Basketball, a longtime favorite at the university, reached a peak in 1988 when the team won the Division II NCAA Championship in a tight game against Alaska-Anchorage. As the clock wound down, the Lowell team held out and claimed a 75-72 victory. Here, the team celebrates with coach Don Doucette. Doucette left Lowell the following year, and the team went into a long decline. (Courtesy of UMass Lowell Athletics Department.)

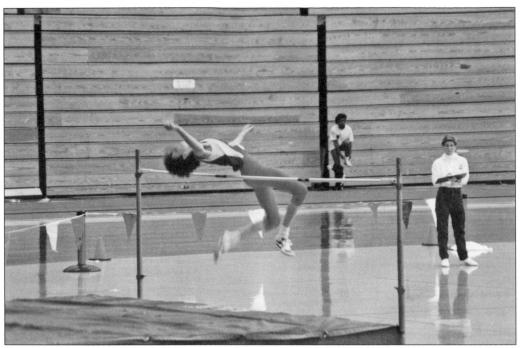

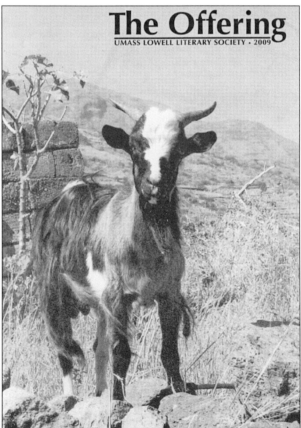

The Offering
UMASS LOWELL LITERARY SOCIETY · 2009

The track and field program continued to excel, but not only in running—Jane Servi saw to that. In 1988, she became the university's first female national champion for her victory in the indoor high-jump championship. She was the only female Lowell athlete to achieve an individual national title until 2007.

Under the aegis of the Literary Society (founded 1989), English department students Paula Haines, Patricia Janice, Judith Dickerman-Nelson, and others resurrected the idea of a literary journal. Titled *The Lowell Pearl*, it included poetry and short stories. In the late 1990s, the name was changed to *The Offering* in honor of the 19th-century mill girl publication *The Lowell Offering*. Haines, now a member of the department, continues to oversee its production.

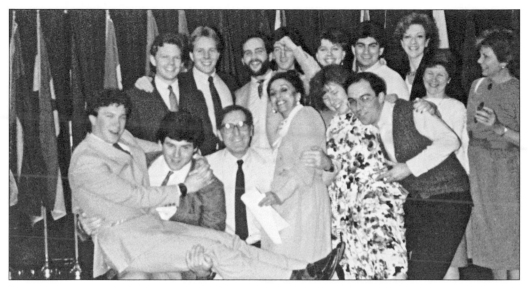

Hired in 1965 and still teaching, Dean Bergeron (history/political science) has influenced countless students with courses like "Radicalism in American History." In 1985, he established the International Relations Club and began student involvement in the Model UN competition. In Model UN, students represent a country and face challenges similar to those faced by official diplomats at the UN. Bergeron is pictured above with the 1986–1987 team that included Roger Cressey (first row, left) and Brian Kenny (second row, left); Cressey is now a nationally recognized counterterrorism analyst who appears on MSNBC, and Kenny was recently appointed chief marketing and communications officer of the Harvard University Business School. In 2007, the University of International Relations in Beijing invited Bergeron to help start a Model UN program there. Pictured below in 2011, the team competed in Turkey. (Courtesy of Dean Bergeron and Jason Carter.)

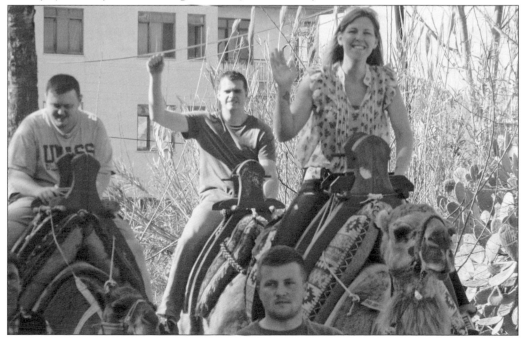

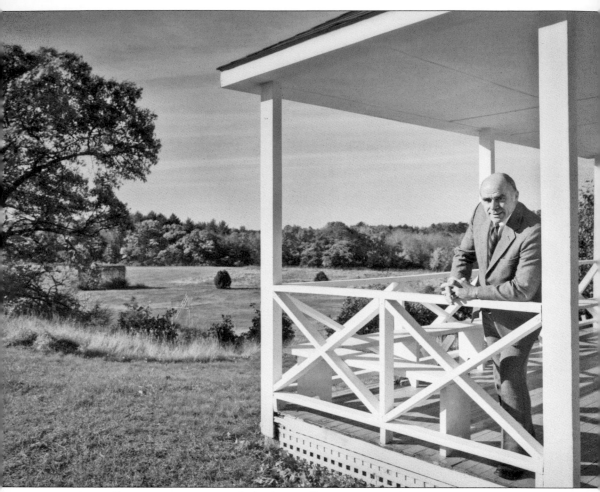

In 1981, William T. Hogan succeeded John Duff as president of the university. Hogan joined the mechanical engineering department in 1963 and served in a number of administrative positions throughout the 1960s and 1970s, including dean of the College of Engineering and vice president for Academic Affairs. As president, Hogan worked to augment the university's standing by earning accreditation for every college and increasing graduate programs. He also tried to overcome the physical and psychological barriers between a "North" and "South" campus by creating the College of Arts and Sciences. In 1991, he oversaw another important merger in the university's history when the University of Lowell became the University of Massachusetts Lowell (UMass Lowell). Hogan served as chancellor of UMass Lowell from 1991 to 2007. He is shown here on the West Campus property owned by the university, located off Princeton Boulevard on the border of Lowell and Chelmsford. (Courtesy of James Higgins.)

Six

MILLENNIUM MANEUVERS

In the new millennium, UMass Lowell has positioned itself for further expansion. The campus has witnessed tremendous growth in its facilities, academic programs, and enrollment. The new campus recreation center (CRC), planned since 1995, officially opened in 2002, and since then, building crews have been evident on both North and South Campuses. (Courtesy of UMass Lowell Office of Public Affairs.)

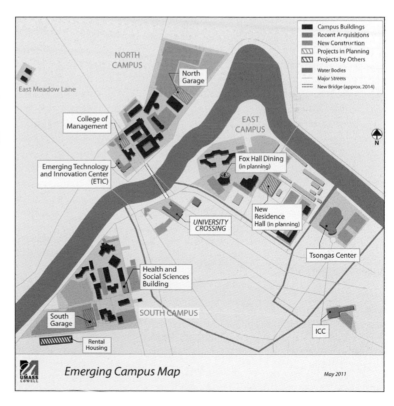

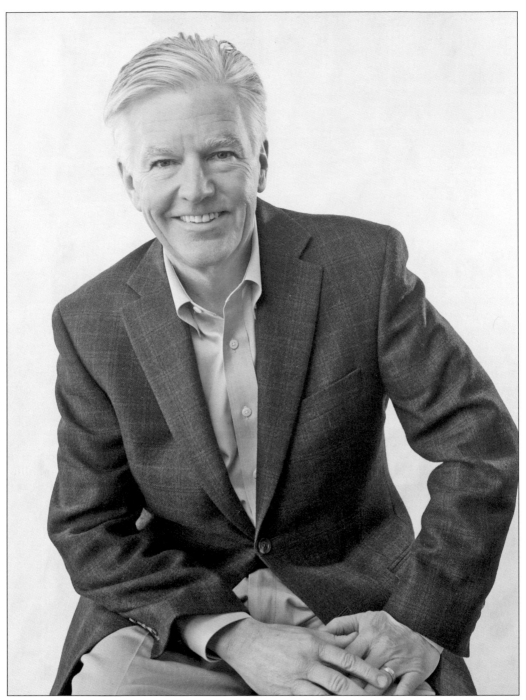

Marty Meehan became chancellor of UMass Lowell in July 2007. He has propelled the school forward in every measure of higher education—academics, research, fundraising, globalization, diversity, campus life, engagement with the community, and the quality of the facilities. A 1978 University of Lowell graduate, Meehan holds a juris doctor of law and a graduate administration degree from Suffolk University. (Courtesy of UMass Lowell Office of Public Affairs and Kevin Harkins.)

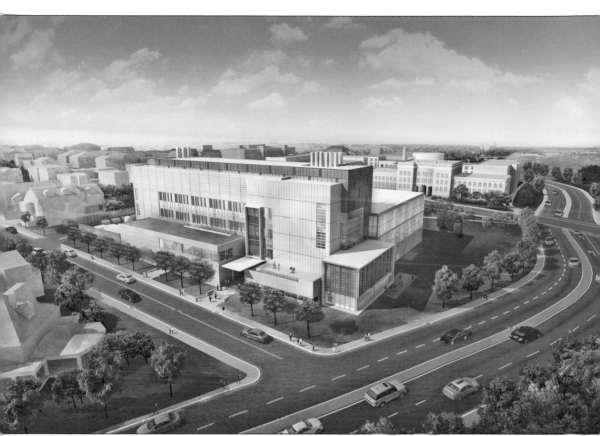

New construction on the North Campus centers on the Emerging Technologies and Innovation Center (ETIC). The 84,000-square-foot research and academic facility will be the hub of industry partnerships and new manufacturing technologies. Construction of the building necessitated the demolition of Smith dormitory. The new building will face Southwick and is slated to open in fall 2012.

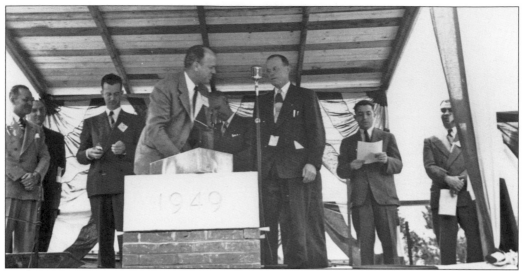

The construction of Smith Hall in 1947 had jump-started Pres. Kenneth Fox's plans to expand the institute in the late 1940s. A number of buildings followed and each one had a cornerstone with a time capsule placed inside (the cornerstone-laying ceremony for Alumni Memorial Library in 1949 is pictured above). During the demolition of Smith Hall in spring 2010, the time capsule was recovered and opened. It contained artifacts related to LTI (student newspapers, a course catalog) as well as letters from school and government officials. Gov. Robert Bradford wrote in his letter: "There are some . . . who insist there is little future left to the world because of the arrival of the atomic age. But I am inclined to disagree . . . I have an idea that when this cornerstone is opened . . . youth will be about the same as it is today—enthusiastic, energetic, courageous and, I am sure, more knowing than ever." (Courtesy of UMass Lowell Public Affairs.)

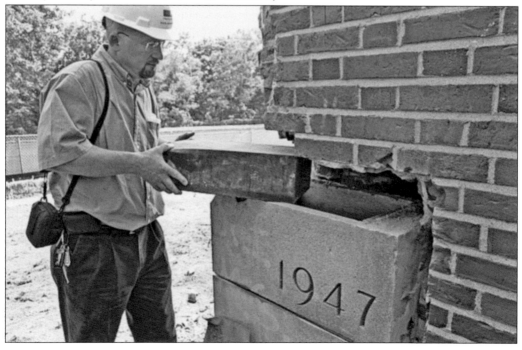

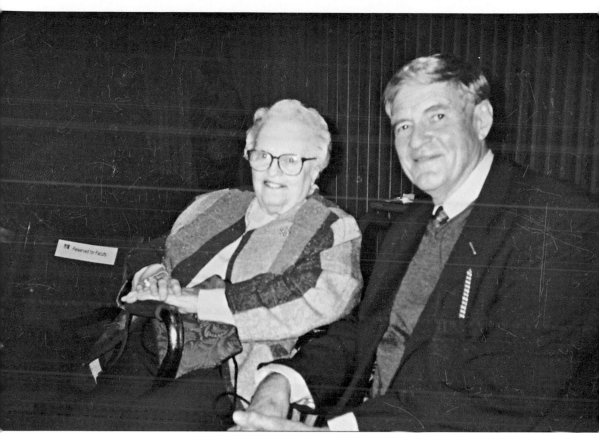

Expansion of the facilities mirrored expansion of the programs. Under Dean Virginia Biggy, the College of Education became an all-graduate school with three doctoral programs. This signaled a culminating moment for an institution that began as a Normal school. Biggy is shown here with prominent educator Theodore Sizer. Biggy received national acclaim for her work on the Reading Rainbow series; she retired in 1989. (Courtesy of Anita Greenwood.)

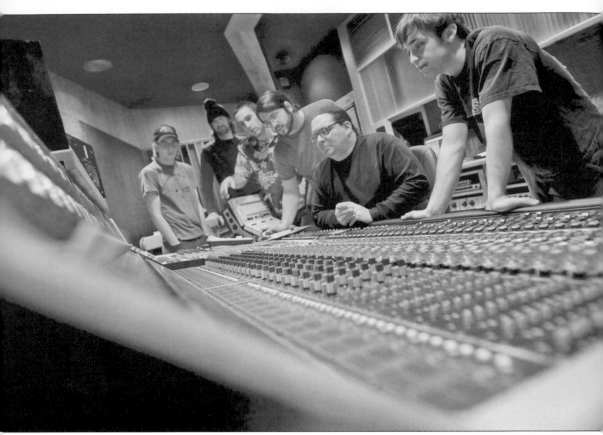

The Sound Recording Technology Program, within the Department of Music, has rapidly grown in national recognition and is one of the few programs of its kind. Students gain both a practical and theoretical foundation for the field. In this image, Asst. Prof. Alex U. Case and a group of students gather around the API Vision Analog Surround Sound Console used for the elective course called Advanced Multitrack Production. (Courtesy of UMass Lowell Office of Public Affairs.)

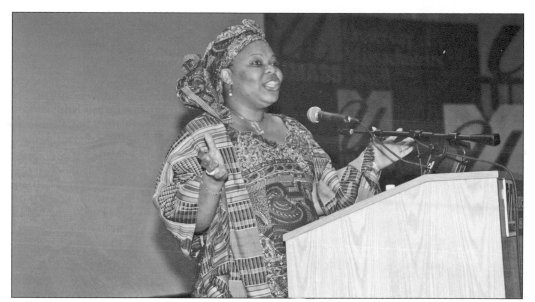

In 2011, Leymah Gbowee received the Greeley Scholar for Peace Studies award from UMass Lowell. Gbowee, an African peace activist and social worker, is the executive director of the Women Peace and Security Network Africa. Her efforts to organize women in Liberia to pray and sing for peace helped end the Liberian Civil War in 2003 and earned Gbowee a Nobel Peace Prize. (Courtesy of Robert Gamache.)

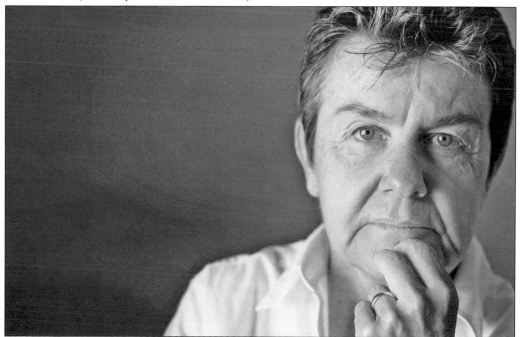

The English department and Center for Arts and Ideas have brought a number of prominent authors to campus. In 2010, Russell Banks and Anita Shreve headlined the first Jack Kerouac Literary Festival, produced with community partners. Kay Ryan (pictured), US Poet Laureate and Pulitzer Prize winner, gave a reading in 2011. Ryan's visit coincided with the addition of a new UMass Lowell concentration in creative writing. (Courtesy of Christina Koci Hernandez.)

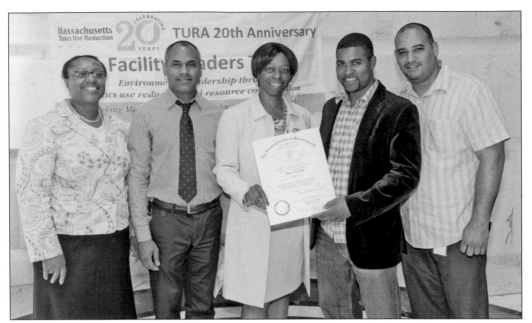

The Toxics Use Reduction Institute (TURI) at UMass Lowell provides resources to protect public health and the environment and to make the Commonwealth a safer and more sustainable place to live and work. The institute's community programming helps businesses and organizations reduce the use of toxic chemicals. The Moreno Auto Body Shop, shown here with members of the Boston Public Health Commission, reduced its use of the solvents toluene and acetone. (Courtesy of TURI.)

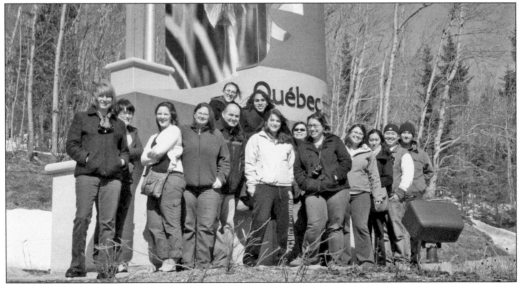

Students with an interest in French can participate in a linguistic immersion program for four days each spring. In partnership with the academic institution CEGEP Beauce-Appalaches, located just south of Quebec in the town of Saint Georges de Beauce, students attend classes and cultural events presented entirely in French. Carole Salmon (Cultural Studies) and Sheila Kirschbaum (Tsongas for Industrial History Center) organize this annual event. (Courtesy of Carole Salmon.)

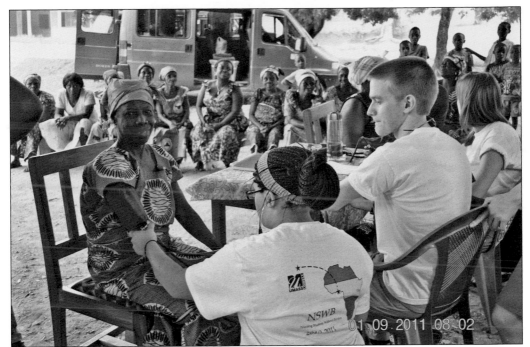

The nursing program started in 1967 under Gertrude Barker. For the last few years, some nursing students have travelled to Ghana. In 2011, UMass Lowell students Alexandra Lamont (back to camera) and Jason Hebert volunteered to take the blood pressure of local residents at a hypertension screening clinic; other students have helped at orphanages in places such as Hohoe. (Courtesy of Valerie King.)

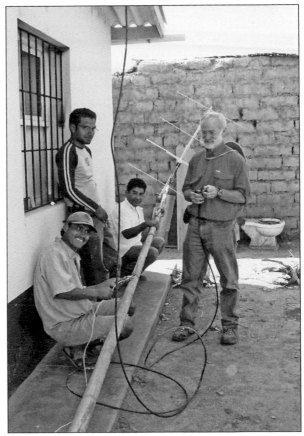

One of the most successful outreach programs at UMass Lowell is the Village Empowerment Project. Begun in 1997 under the direction of Prof. John Duffy (right), students and volunteers travel to Peru twice a year. There, they team up with local residents to design and install sustainable systems that include solar panels, water pumping and purification, and transceiver radios for remote clinics and schools. The project has already installed 90 systems in 50 villages. (Courtesy of John Duffy.)

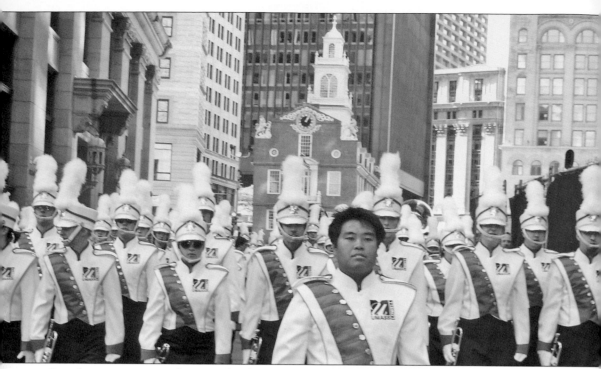

On a breezy evening, the sounds of the UMass Lowell marching band fill the surrounding neighborhoods. Started in 1979, the band has earned a notable reputation throughout the Northeast and has played for President Clinton and Massachusetts governors William Weld, Paul Celucci, and Deval Patrick. Band members are drawn from all colleges, fusing university-wide talent into one ensemble. (Courtesy of Debra-Nicole Huber.)

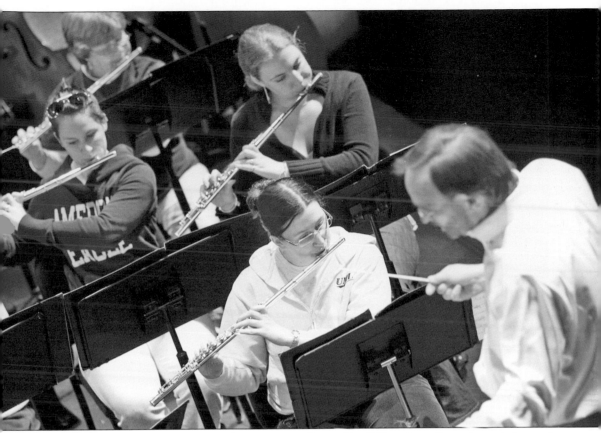

In addition to an annual season of concerts performed by UMass Lowell students (pictured here), the music department also hosts internationally acclaimed performers. In 2011, classical guitar virtuoso Eliot Fisk gave a free concert and conducted a master class. The Harlem Quartet visited the semester prior as part of the UMass Lowell String Project. (Courtesy of Center for Arts and Ideas.)

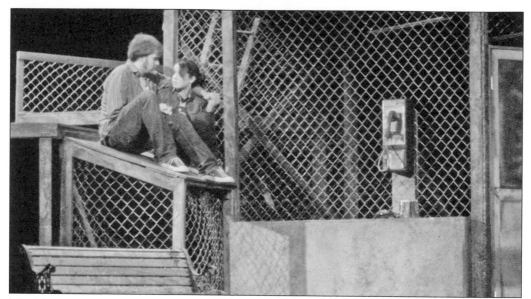

The Theater Arts Program collaborates with the student drama club, the Off-Broadway Players, to provide riveting productions throughout the year. In this photograph, students Zack Tretheway (class of 2011) and Kate Munoz (class of 2014) perform a scene from Eric Bogosian's *SubUrbia*. The long tradition of interest in the dramatic arts, demonstrated at both the Normal School and the Textile School, culminated in 2010 with the inception of a Theater Arts major.

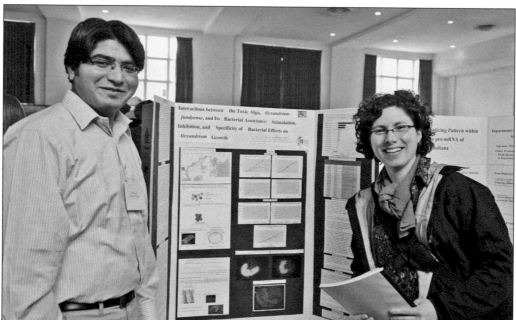

The university instituted the Undergraduate Student Research Symposium in 1998 to share the innovative collaborative research projects undertaken by students and faculty. Students display research through presentations on themed panels, or put together poster sessions. For the 2007 symposium, Nilesh Pande (left) worked with faculty advisor Juliette Rooney-Varga on the causes of "red tide" in coastal New England. (Courtesy of Robert Gamache.)

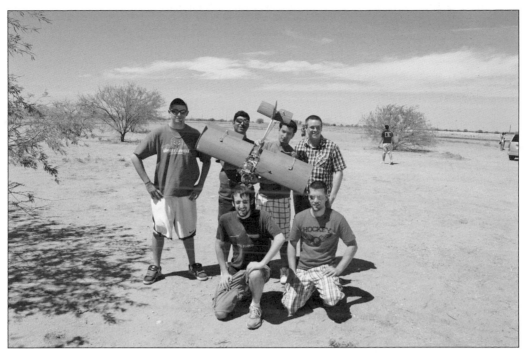

Members of the student chapter of the American Institute of Aeronautics and Astronautics competed in the spring 2010 Design/Build/Fly competition for the first time as an individual university entry. The team designed and built a suitcase-portable unmanned aerial vehicle for the event, held in Tuscon, Arizona. Pictured here are, from left to right, (first row) Bradford Olson and Daniel Desjadin; (second row) Robert Barger, Abdelwahed Nabat, Gabriel Abreu, and John Miniter. (Courtesy of David Willis.)

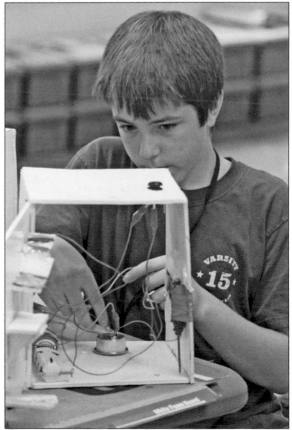

Every summer since 2000, UMass Lowell has offered DESIGNCAMP, a science and engineering summer program aimed at students in the 5th to 10th grades. Each workshop runs for a week, and students can choose from a variety of projects, including sea mobiles, carnival contraptions, crime science, or inventions and gizmos. (Courtesy of Michael Penta.)

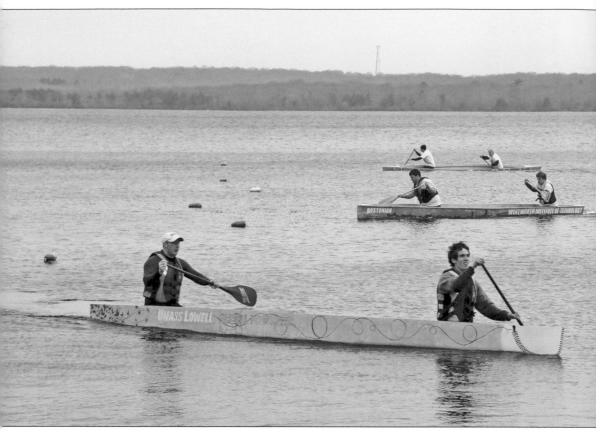

In an event that seems to defy the laws of physics, students participate each spring in the National Concrete Canoe Competition sponsored by the American Society of Civil Engineers. The concrete canoes must float while full of water. At the 2011 Northeast Regionals, UMass Lowell students Brian Allard (left) and Brian Foley placed second in the two-man sprints. UMass Lowell placed third in the overall competition. (Courtesy of John Ting.)

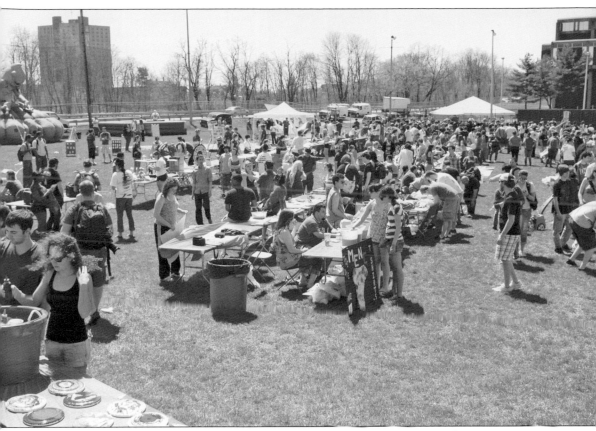

One of the social highlights for students on campus is Spring Carnival. Held on the playing fields of either North or South Campus, the carnival includes games and events; many of the student clubs also set up tables to raise funds for their organizations. Nine times out of 10, it rains on the scheduled day, but 2011, pictured here, was a welcome exception. (Courtesy of Mike Mizzoni.)

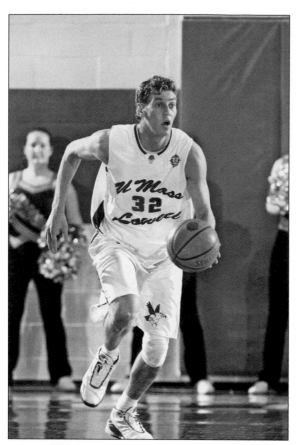

After a long losing period, in 2001 and 2002 the men's basketball team made it to the NCAA Division II tournament for the first since 1988. In 2003 and 2004, the team won the regional championships. A driving force behind this success was forward Elad Inbar, who remains the university's all-time leading scorer with 2,099 career points. After graduation, Inbar returned to his native Israel to play professional basketball. (Courtesy of UMass Lowell Athletics Department.)

In 2009, all eyes turned toward the hockey team. In this image, Maury Edwards (No. 7) celebrates with Chris Auger (No. 16) after the program's biggest win of the last few years—Auger had just scored the game-winning overtime goal against Northeastern University in the 2009 Hockey East Tournament Semifinals at the Boston Garden. (Courtesy of UMass Lowell Athletics Department.)

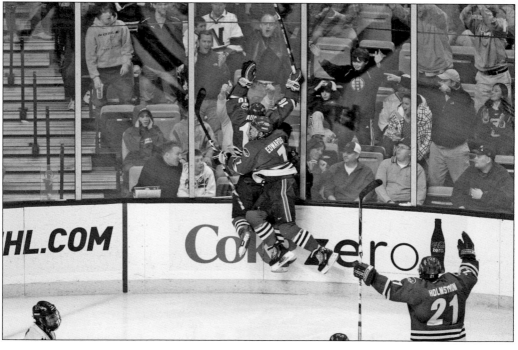

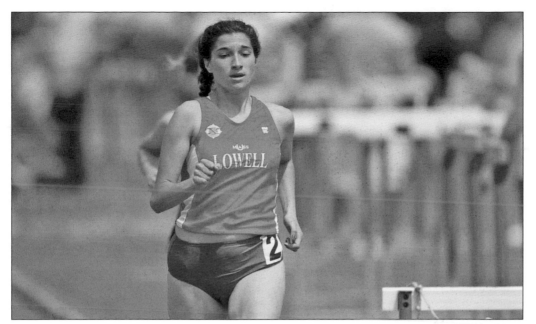

Nicole Plante has the honor of being UMass Lowell's most decorated female athlete. She crowned her college career with an NCAA Division II victory in the 10,000-meter event in 2007, making her UMass Lowell's first-ever outdoor track and field national champion. Plante's victory literally set the ball rolling—in 2010, Jacqui Barrett became the next female student to win a national championship with a 50-foot, 8.25-inch throw in the shot put competition.

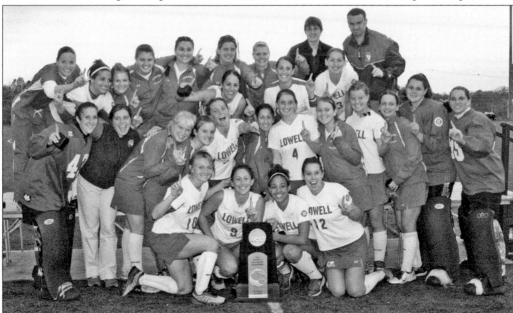

Women's field hockey soared to national attention in the early 2000s. Under coach Shannon Hlebichuk, the team reached the NCAA Division II finals and semifinals in 2003 and 2004. In 2005, UMass Lowell won its first NCAA Championship match in a dramatic double-overtime victory over Bloomsburg University. The team continued to grow in depth and won the championship again in 2009. (Courtesy of UMass Lowell Athletics Department.)

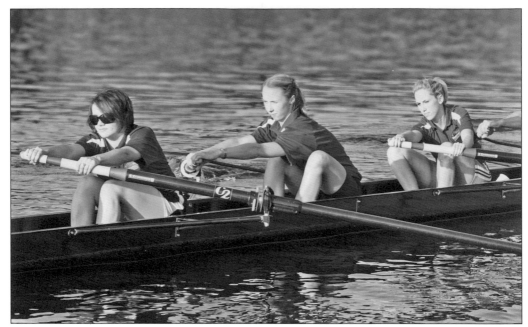

The rowing program has continued to grow in the wake of Shelagh Donohoe's success. In May 2010, women's rowing was officially elevated to varsity status as a NCAA Division II sport. The boathouse, located about half-mile upriver from the campus, received a substantial renovation the same year. Renamed the UMass Lowell Bellegarde Boathouse, it was originally constructed in 1982 and named for Lowell boater Edmund Bellegarde. Donohoe praised UMass Lowell's efforts: "I've rowed all over the world and the Merrimack is still one of my favorite rivers. I think they have all the resources they need for a successful program, an incredible river and a great high school program. The natural resources between the river and the community are what will make the program successful. You can't just put a rowing program anywhere." (Courtesy of UMass Lowell Athletics Department.)

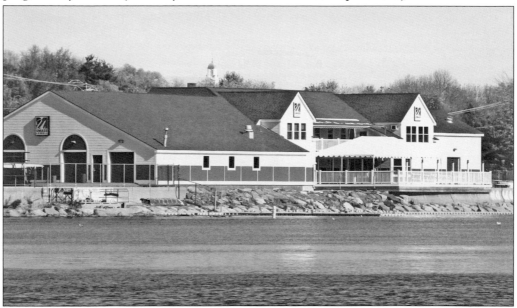

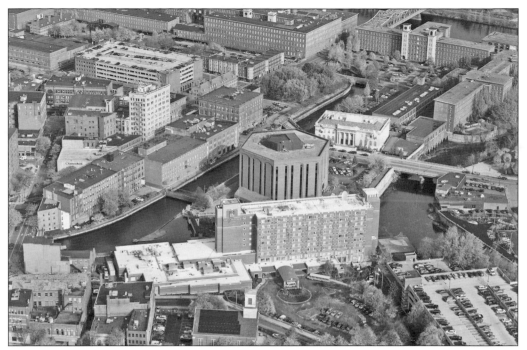

As part of continuing efforts to build partnerships with the city of Lowell, the university purchased the former Doubletree Hotel in the heart of downtown and converted it into a 400-bed dormitory and conference center. Now known as the Inn & Conference Center (ICC), the building is ideally situated near the Lower Locks of the Pawtucket Canal. (Courtesy of James Higgins.)

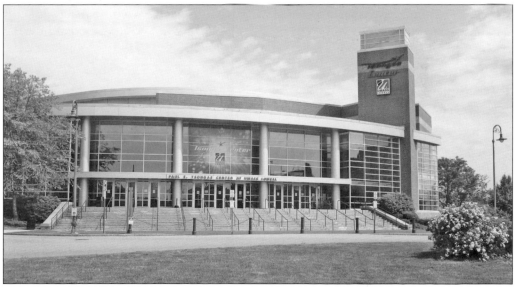

The university's facilities expanded in 2010 with the acquisition of the Tsongas Arena in downtown Lowell. Previously operated by the City of Lowell, the university will use it for the hockey team's home games as well as concerts, commencements, and other university events. The building, named for the late Sen. Paul E. Tsongas, is now known as the Tsongas Center at UMass Lowell. (Courtesy of Marie Frank.)

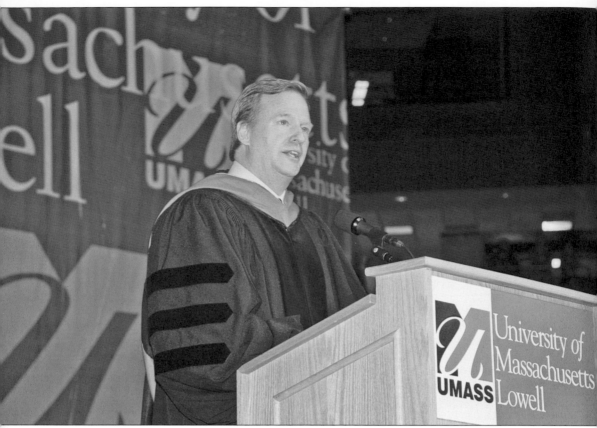

National Football League commissioner Robert Goodell served as the May 2010 commencement speaker, addressing a record number of nearly 2,400 graduates. Goodell welcomed "the opportunity to share . . . how the lessons I've learned from my father and leading the NFL can be applied to anything they pursue in life." Goodell accepted a posthumous doctor of humane letters degree for his father, the late US senator Charles Goodell. (Courtesy of UMass Lowell Office of Public Affairs.)

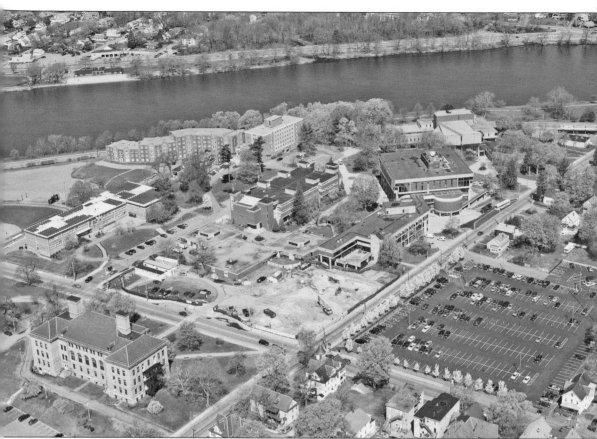

This 2011 aerial photograph of South Campus offers an informative comparison with the earlier aerials of the 1950s. The campus occupies the entire neighborhood between Broadway and Wilder Streets, a faculty parking lot occupies the site of the former Lovejoy residence, and the student parking lot occupies the space of the demolished cotton mill. Sheehy dormitory, named for former state senator Paul Sheehy of Lowell, snakes down the ridge toward the river behind Concordia dormitory at the top of the photograph. (Courtesy of James Higgins.)

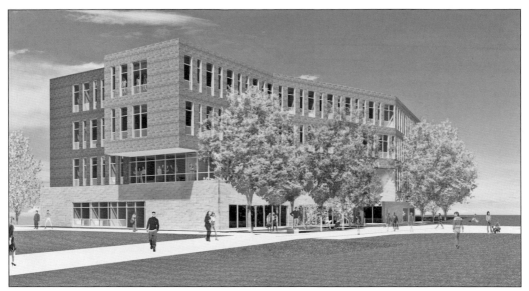

The new Health and Social Sciences building marks the first new construction on South Campus in more than 30 years. Situated on the prominent corner of Broadway and Wilder Streets, it will provide instructional space and faculty offices for the criminal justice and criminology, nursing, and psychology departments and is expected to open in the spring of 2013. (Courtesy of UMass Lowell Office of Public Affairs.)

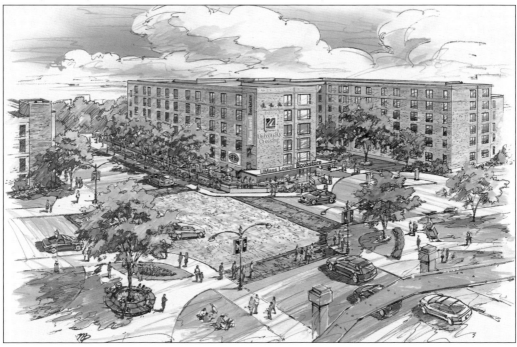

In January 2010, the university acquired the former St. Joseph's Hospital in Lowell. This complex will provide much-needed space for a student body that has seen a 30 percent increase in undergraduates in the past three years. Named "University Crossing," it will offer an important connection between the university's three campuses and the downtown district, all located within walking distance. (Courtesy of UMass Lowell Office of Public Affairs.)

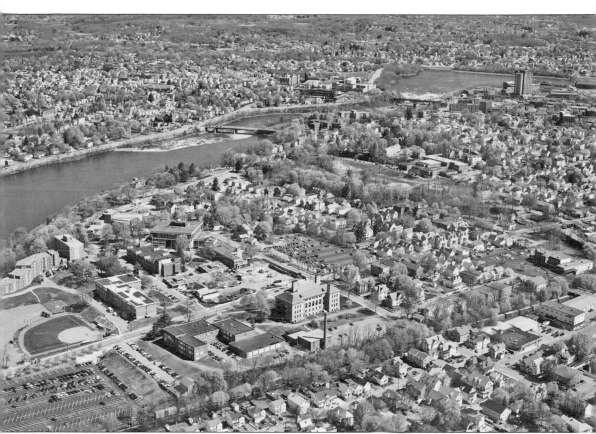

The Merrimack River has been the spine of Lowell's existence. The early industrialists chose this bend in the river as the site for mill buildings and began the city's role in the American Industrial Revolution. Without the river, there would have been no Lowell, and without Lowell, no need for the Normal School or the Textile School. It is highly fitting that the two schools that served as the basis for UMass Lowell flank the great river. Just as the textiles and technology of Lowell's industry flowed from the city to all corners of the world, the students, programs, and endeavors of the university will continue to carry forth its mission. (Courtesy of James Higgins.)

DISCOVER THOUSANDS OF LOCAL HISTORY BOOKS FEATURING MILLIONS OF VINTAGE IMAGES

Arcadia Publishing, the leading local history publisher in the United States, is committed to making history accessible and meaningful through publishing books that celebrate and preserve the heritage of America's people and places.

Find more books like this at
www.arcadiapublishing.com

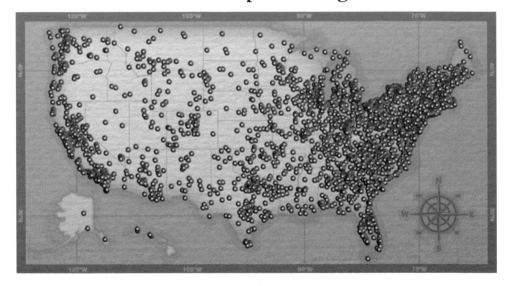

Search for your hometown history, your old stomping grounds, and even your favorite sports team.

Consistent with our mission to preserve history on a local level, this book was printed in South Carolina on American-made paper and manufactured entirely in the United States. Products carrying the accredited Forest Stewardship Council (FSC) label are printed on 100 percent FSC-certified paper.

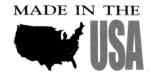